MY WILDERNESS IN BLOOM

MY
WILDERNESS
IN BLOOM

Phil Drabble

MICHAEL JOSEPH – LONDON

With my love
to
JESS
who shares the problems
as well as the pleasures
of persuading our
wilderness to bloom

First published in Great Britain by Michael Joseph Ltd
27 Wrights Lane, Kensington, London W8 5DZ
1986
Reprinted 1987

British Library Cataloguing in Publication Data
Drabble, Phil
My wilderness in bloom.
1. Natural areas—England—
Staffordshire
I. Title
639.9'09424'6   QH77.G7

ISBN 0-7181-2691-2

Filmset by BAS Printers Limited, Over Wallop, Hampshire
Printed and bound in Italy by Mondadori, Verona.

CONTENTS

FOREWORD

by the Honourable William Waldegrave, MP,

Minister of State for the Environment,
Countryside and Local Government.

The conservation movement comprises a broad church. And if government policies represent the high Anglicanism of the movement, Phil Drabble represents the Non-conformists. The analogy is apt, since love of and concern for nature is not confined to any one sector of society. People who hunt and shoot, farmers, foresters, ecologists – even politicians and bureaucrats – all care about our wild flora and fauna. Of course they all have differing views about the best ways in which we can conserve the beauty and variety of the wildlife of this country. The differences among them are many and the arguments fierce. This is as it should be; the one certainty is that, as long as there is debate and argument, we know there are many who care about and are alert to the pressures on our countryside.

Phil Drabble here presents a personal testament. It is one man's perception, drawn from direct experience, of both the why and the how of conservation. He touches, rightly in my view, on the distinction between conservation and preservation, on the need to accept change and evolution. He shows what *can* be done, but sensibly avoids the dogmatism of what *should* be done. He accepts that there is no magic overall formula.

It is certainly possible to disagree with some of the sentiments expressed. But the basic concept of Phil Drabble's approach – that individuals should themselves endeavour to foster richness and variety of wildlife in however small an area – must be right. More fundamentally, every word in this book makes clear that Phil Drabble cares. So should we all.

N

| 0 | 100 yd | ⅛ ml | ¼ ml |
| 0 | 100m | ¼ km |

PRIMROSE DELL

New yard
Sett

Field Maple

Ley
Close

MIDDLE POOL
New sett

NEW RIDE

SOFTWOODS

Reserve boundary

SOFTWOODS

Patch
thinned

Gorse Patch

Cockshutt

Close

Fence

Heronry

HARDWOODS

Wild Service Tree

DAFFODIL LAWN

Holly Covert

Lords Coppice
CHRISTMAS TREES

Fence

SOFTWOODS

Long Lands

Deer
Glade

Working ride for timber extraction

Fox earth

DUNSTAL
POOL

House sett

Dunstalpool

Plantation

NEW RIDE

MIDDLE RIDE

Paddock

GOAT
LODGE

Drive

Reserve boundary

←Drive to Farm

PLAN
OF
RESERVE

Spinney

Paddock

Greenhouse   Kitchen ga

Ha ha

Lawn

Shrubs and
flowers

Lawn

Hornbeam hedge   Village

Pump yard
Out buildings
Corn store
Gate to paddock
Tractor shed

Gate   Terrace   Yew
hedge

GOAT LODGE

Log hovel

Path to wood

Pen

Hen run

Dog
paddock

Yard

Garage

Front
Lawns

Drive

To Farm

ENLARGED DETAIL O
LODGE AND GARDEN

PREFACE

Twenty-odd years in the engineering industry were more than enough for me, so my wife Jess and I decided to do what so many of our friends only dream about. We bought a clapped-out cottage, buried at the edge of a wood deep in the countryside, and I set out to earn my living with my pen.

The motive, at first, was to escape from a world of accelerating change, where next day was unpredictable and security was unknown. The reward was all we had hoped for because we found ourselves living, all year round, with wildlife and surroundings we had known only on holiday before.

By adapting techniques used by the gamekeepers of my boyhood, I discovered that it was possible to encourage selected animals and birds at the expense of species which did them harm; in 1968, our wood was designated a Site of Special Scientific Interest, and in European Conservation Year, 1970, it earned a Countryside Award.

Since those days, SSSIs have become a trendy jargon term because 'advances' in farming techniques have destroyed so many important habitats for wildlife that it has become necessary to protect much of what remains by law.

Few would quarrel with that, but the countryside has been evolving since time began, and nobody yet has been able to bring change to a halt. Protecting parts of it, as official nature reserves and sites of interest to scientists, is, at best, cosmetic surgery which can only scratch skin deep. Since precious few of us are lucky enough to own land that has not changed for centuries, few ordinary people can be involved directly.

But thousands own odd bits of countryside, like mine, which is of little economic or amenity value but which could give sanctuary to a wide variety of plants, animals and birds, if managed carefully. Hordes of keen, amateur naturalists could contribute as much as, or more than, officialdom by managing their own small sites for the benefit of threatened species.

Although they will need encouragement and advice, their efforts need cost the taxpayer nothing – and this book describes my own efforts to practise what I preach.

ACKNOWLEDGEMENTS

All photographs are by Harry Avery except the following:

G. I. Bernard: page 190; *Birmingham Post & Mail*: page 53; Alan Goodger (courtesy of Natural Selection): page 95; David T. Grewcock: page 125; Hunters of Chester: page 181; E. A. Janes: page 179; Derek Johnson: pages 21, 46, 110 (top left), 166, 219; Geoffrey Kinns (Natural Selection): 10, 47, 70, 86 (bottom), 155, 194, 195, 203, 207; Iain Malin (Natural Selection): page 23 (left); R. P. Lawrence: page 192; Brian Moody: facing forword, 222; Paul Morrison: pages 138, 142, 147 (main photo and top inset photo); Walter Murray: page 154; W. S. Paton (Natural Selection): page 14; Stanley Porter: pages 25, 33, 36, 44, 56 (bottom), 58, 59, 60, 79, 80, 85, 93, 101, 106, 108, 113, 129, 153, 161, 162, 164, 188, 208; Stanley Porter (now the copyright of RSPB): pages 49; 77, 97, 144, 145, 172, 189, 201, 221; Gerald Springthorpe: page 62, 64; Wilkins Photography: pages 31 (main photo), 38, 214; J. F. Young (Natural Selection): pages 69, 74. The author and publishers would like to thank all the above for their kind permission to use their photographs in this book. Map by Boris Weltman.

1. HOME TERRITORY

I am as territorial as a badger, preferring the undistinguished modesty of my own wood to other men's estates, however glamorous. This is made immediately obvious by the two small wire-netting enclosures in the paddock, half way between our windows and the woodland edge. They started life as chicken runs and outspoken friends describe them as eyesores which make the place look like a fourth-rate poultry farm.

Such criticism doesn't impress us because those two wire-netting frames provide endless pleasure, beginning at dusk and continuing, on and off, long after night has fallen. They are illuminated, after dark, by a small electric floodlight fixed in an adjacent oak tree and, when they are occupied, the television screen starts talking to itself because all eyes are fixed on the figures in the frames.

There is no doubt about their identity because the burly, grey-coated figures, with white striped heads, are obviously badgers. They appear, at first sight, to have walked into a cage trap, about four feet long by two feet wide, and it is indeed baited as a trap would be, though wild horses would not drag the recipe from me, lest less scrupulous imitators use it in traps from which escape is impossible. My only purpose for placing the lure in wire-netted security is to prevent the deer in the wood from nicking it before the badgers come.

But I have to do more than that. I have to cover the food with heavy tiles to keep it safe from tits during the day. When the badgers arrive, they treat such safeguards with contempt, and send the tiles spinning with powerful feet, more used to excavating setts in stony soil.

Every night – or almost every night, for badgers are far less predictable than so-called experts pretend – they emerge from the House Sett behind the rhododendron thicket, amble across the turf towards the Lodge, dive through the entrance of the 'chicken coop' and delight us by feasting, oblivious of the voyeurs behind the window pane.

This couldn't have happened when we bought the wood almost a quarter of a century ago because, although badgers foraged here occasionally, there was not an occupied sett in the wood and certainly there were no badgers bold enough to come so close to human habitation, lit brightly enough to turn night to day. Our sojourn here has hammered home the fact that wildlife is less disturbed by artificial light or mechanical disturbance than by unpredictable or unusual human activity. There would obviously be fewer mangled corpses on our roads if hedgehogs and badgers, rabbits, squirrels and hares appreciated that rumbling tyres and dazzling headlights were the harbingers of doom.

Long before we managed to seduce the badgers by our hospitality, the fallow deer had become confident enough to leave the wood and venture into the paddock to scrump any spilled grain the pheasants left, or flaked maize or monkey nuts tipped uneaten from the feeders hung for tits and nuthatches. When we arrived, it was a red-letter day just to see the fleeting shadow of a fallow deer,

Goat Lodge across Dunstal Pool, frozen but peaceful

The fallow deer continue to chew their cud contentedly when we pass

melting into the undergrowth. Now we see them every day, at close enough quarters to identify them individually.

There is no magic about this for the secret is security. Wildlife thrives just as we do when it feels that tomorrow will really come, so the creatures which share our wood have learned, by slow experience, that far from wishing them harm, we are their allies.

Jess and I bought the place originally to escape some of the mad pressures of artificial, urban life so that I could earn our bread and butter with my pen and, although I cram more hours' work into the day than I ever did, the rewards have more than compensated.

I am out in the wood whenever I can and Jess accompanies me at least once or twice a day — and the dogs never miss the opportunity. It might be thought that two people, with two dogs, would be more than enough to scare all shy creatures to the far end of the parish, but it seems that almost the reverse is true. We wander quietly and continuously and we don't chatter. We keep closely together and we stick to the maze of paths and rides I have carved through the trees over the years. This is not to mollycoddle our decrepitude, but to allow us to move quietly and, above all, predictably.

It is quite astonishing how quickly wildlife recognises and falls in with regular habits. Deer, lying down to chew their cud, soon realise that two familiar figures, even with two dogs at heel, will pass by harmlessly within a few yards, or even feet. They stop munching for a few seconds, and prepare for instant getaway, but they do not convert the plan to action without good cause. So long as we

The deer come right up to the house to feed; the wire-net frame in which the badgers feed can be seen in the background

I place food under tiles which the badgers fling aside when they emerge at dusk

do not stop in our tracks or catch their eye by staring directly at them, they regard us as harmless as a flock of rooks regard the immobility of a familiar scarecrow. So, by wandering round, choosing different paths each time, we have got to know the habitat and its inhabitants as familiar friends – and they return the compliment.

Lords Coppice, in the south-eastern corner of the wood, has row upon row of Christmas trees, planted over a period of three years. We harvested the first thousand in the autumn of 1985, to raise the wind for preventing the pool in Primrose Dell from drying up (*see* page 168). The space where the Christmas trees came from is thickening up with briar which, whatever one thinks of bramble patches, is a vast improvement on the sterile pines that were there for more than twenty years. We shall eat the blackberries, or some of them. The deer will browse the leaves and, with luck, a wide variety of birds and butterflies will make their homes there.

When Jess and I were up there yesterday, we saw three woodcock, and I know of no more magical experience than watching woodcock roding on summer nights. As dusk falls, the bird flies a predetermined course, usually along the woodland rides, repeating his route time and again, and uttering a throaty cry. His wings appear to move more slowly than such flight demands because the bird travels deceptively fast, propelled by deliberate, slowish wingbeats; as he flies, he repeats a low croak, interspersed by a much higher, creaking note.

I love being quite alone in the wood to watch woodcock, for it sings of changeless time which gives confidence that, if such rituals went on in the long-distant past, and continue now, there is room for confidence in the future. It set the pattern for what we wanted to accomplish in our tenure of the wood – to leave it with a chance of continuity.

2. THE INCURABLE ITCH

Microchips and automation, easy transport and increased leisure have resulted in a tidal wave of pressures, sweeping people back to the countryside. Most of us are allergic to change, especially when it is beyond our control, so that we suffer from the rose-tinted delusion that we might shed our insecurity if we could escape from the urban rat-race to Rip Van Winkle-land.

I know the feeling because I spent a happy childhood among the industrial dereliction on the edge of Staffordshire's Black Country. Although the scenery would have turned the stomachs of most modern environmentalists, there were more crested newts in the swags, or subsidence pools, than in plenty of nature reserves which are now designated Sites of Special Scientific Interest. There were goldfinches among the thistles, elephant hawk moths bred in the rosebay willowherb and rabbit warrens pockmarked the colliery spoil banks. The scenery may not have been very up-market, but I grew up with a wonderful working dog as my companion, and instinctively acquired the taste for traditional rural pursuits. Although it was unlikely habitat, for an embryo naturalist, it sustained a surprising spectrum of wildlife. When the time came to earn my living, I got a job in a factory which anchored me in urban surroundings and subjected me to all the competitive pressures from which it is now fashionable to pine to escape.

Like plenty of my modern counterparts, I took my holidays in country places – but I was more committed than just that. Daylight permitting, I was out with my dog before I went to work and again when I came home; I went ferreting for rats or rabbits every Sunday – but I couldn't afford a cottage in the country during the tough, competitive era immediately after the war. Perhaps that enforced confinement has given me sympathy with the urban throng which now invades the countryside, and has driven home the point that the wildlife which still survives needs protection from those who love it as well as from those who would harm it deliberately – for sport or, accidentally, for profit.

My good news then was that kestrels nested in the disused workshops of the West Bromwich factory where I served what seemed a life sentence of twenty-three years. The industrial squalor of the canal banks outside the factory provided rich pickings for voles and mice and rats which, in turn, made up the menu of the kestrels. They accepted urban life more easily than I did.

Deep as the instinct was to migrate to a more congenial life and surroundings, a practical streak kept my nose to the grindstone until I had accumulated a little capital to keep me afloat if things did not go to plan when the time came to make a change. For my last sixteen years in industry, I wrote books and broadcast as a hobby, making enough friends on the media Old Boy network to give me a fair chance of getting enough commissions to earn a living with my pen. I was acutely conscious that Jess and I would go hungry for necessities and thirsty for luxuries if my ink ran dry.

Directors in industry are often paid more than they are worth so, in 1961,

Kestrels are just as fond of wild country as urban wasteland

when I was forty-seven and after seven years on the board of a fairly large company, we had pouched enough to take the risk of opting for a simpler life. I shook the dust of commerce off my shoes and swapped them for a pair of welly boots.

We soon discovered that it is by no means as simple as it sounds to get the sort of cottage in the country that we wanted. Our last house, on the edge of the commuter belt, had been a half-timbered Elizabethan farmhouse, with a pool fed by the millstream, and ten acres of paddock and orchard. It looked quite imposing although it was called the Cottage and was just the sort of place estate agents drool about, but we soon discovered that, by the time we had stopped the roof leaking, cut out the dry rot in the floors and swatted the woodworm in the rafters, it was time to start again.

Neighbours' cats had poached the pigeons, their kids had scrumped the apples, and grey squirrels had stolen the walnuts before they were ripe. We nearly had the paddock confiscated by compulsory purchase for a school playing-field and

The Cottage was ancient, beautiful – and expensive to keep up

the network of surrounding footpaths put time-bombs under any chance of privacy. We discovered that 'a cottage in the country' may provide no more seclusion than a villa in suburbia but usually entails the added hassle of a twenty-mile trek to and from the office in the daily rush hours. At least we knew some of the pitfalls to avoid.

I have described in *My Beloved Wilderness* how we searched for our elusive ideal, only to find snags ranging from cellars full of water to land let to shooting syndicates. When we did find the perfect place, which was in the middle of a great estate, luck was on our side because the estate was on the market and likely to be fragmented. Otherwise, it would have been most unlikely that anyone would sell a cottage to a stranger if he still enjoyed the amenities of the land surrounding it. That was the good news.

The bad news was that before the estate was sold to some property speculators whose assets were held in the Bahamas, the heir to the estate decided to withdraw the Lodge from the sale; as an added complication he lived in Australia. After acquiring the estate, the property tycoons were soon selling it off in lots to the highest bidders – and they owned the piece of woodland we had our eye on. To add to our problems, the paddock and pool in front of the Lodge belonged to a neighbouring farmer.

Those who have moved house even once will be aware that it is not always easy to get the small print in the contract agreed so the deal can be concluded. The problems of persuading two owners, who were not keen to sell anyway, and a third who was always capable of snatching the pen out of my hand if anyone offered a penny more, will haunt me for ever, but hardfaced persistence triumphed in the end.

By the end of 1963, we were the optimistic owners of a derelict lodge, with no mod cons, approached by a pot-holed drive and lane to the main road a mile away.

Next to the Lodge was Holly Covert, the last bit of woodland standing in Bagot's Wood which had originally sprawled across almost 1000 acres and was a relic of the ancient Forest of Needwood. The rest had been asset-stripped by a succession of landowners without direct heirs to whom they might have wished to leave a viable inheritance. Although the land could not be sold, the timber could be harvested as any other normal crop could be. So there was nothing to stop an owner chopping down the trees and cashing in on the proceeds. The snag was that the licence permitting the trees to be felled specified that the cleared land must be replanted and, in this case, the land had been leased to the Forestry Commission for 999 years at half a crown an acre. This produced the princely rent of £2.40 a week for 1000 acres, making the land virtually worthless.

It is an ill wind that blows nobody any good, for about half the timber on the land we had bought had also been sold and leased to the Forestry Commission on the same terms, reducing the value to suit our pocket, so that the whole place came ridiculously cheap because the Lodge was a ruin and the woodland almost worthless commercially or even scenically. For better or worse, there was no doubt that we had succeeded in 'getting away from it all'!

e were careful to preserve the iginal Lodge as it had always en, adding our extension obtrusively at the back

3. HISTORIC STICK

The Walking Stick Oak says it all – with the same sincerity, the same bias, and the same illusions as modern well-meaning folk who delude themselves that we can preserve the countryside for ever, without change. Even in its decrepitude, the great tree cuts the most expensive combine harvester down to size. The flamboyant gadgetry may be modern as tomorrow now, but the Walking Stick will still be standing when the combine has collapsed into a heap of rusting scrap.

The great tree is unique because it stands over seventy feet to its lowest branch, a veritable giant among the most majestic oaks. Significantly, for those who chase the moonbeams of a changeless countryside, the Walking Stick Oak is dead. It stands on the rise above our wood as the last gaunt memorial to the magnificent oaks for which the deer park was once famous, and to a line of landowners who have long since returned to dust. Old survey maps of the estate pinpoint the sites of other famous trees which achieved immortality, if only on paper, by being recorded individually on the Ordnance Survey map.

The most famous of all was Beggar's Oak, a stunted monster of immense girth, but only knee-high to the Walking Stick. Even in the ancient past, the cavern of its belly was large enough to shelter strangers who trespassed in the park. Legend goes that a beggar, cowering there, once asked in vain for alms from Lord Bagot, the landowner, who passed by, stony faced. The beggar crept back into the hollow tree's shelter to die and, with his last breath, he cursed the Bagot family, praying that, when the oak collapsed, they would suffer a similar fate. Whether from prudence or a guilty conscience, instructions were given that the Beggar's Oak should receive the utmost care and, when its branches creaked with age, they were propped up with great sprags so that its life was prolonged unnaturally. But, within months of its final collapse, the estate was broken up and the proceeds passed to a cousin in Australia who in turn sold it to the property speculators based in the Bahamas.

Also on the map were the King and Queen Oaks – though I know not which kings or queens they commemorated – the Venison Oak and the Squitch Oak. The latter dominated Squitch Bank which when I first knew it was arid, inedible squitch, as its name implied, but is now a golden prairie of waving corn – for better or for worse.

At the same time that the property speculators sold the corner where our Lodge stands to Jess and me, they flogged 1000 acres of park to Brian Dale, a Shropshire millionaire, for £60,000 and I gather they chucked in almost 1000 acres of Bagot's Wood for good measure. The price of good farmland in these parts is now more than £2000 an acre so that £60 an acre at public auction even twenty years ago gives a fair idea of what it was thought to be worth. Even at that price, however, local farmers thought he was mad. The parkland consisted of feg and rush grass, covered with thistles thick enough to blow a summer snowstorm of dainty thistledown, and interspersed by ancient stag-headed oaks.

Jess, who is a dedicated gardener, breathes curses even more horrific than the oak-bound tramp on all who harbour such weeds which seed onto her lawn and garden. But the thistles up in the park soon vanished because millionaires do not make their millions by allowing sentiment to interfere with business.

Corn could not be grown on the feggy parkland for the simple reason that it was impossible to plough because of the scattered oak trees, roots where trees had stood previously, and the lack of any artificial drainage. So Mr Dale's first job was to bring in a bulldozer with a steel hawser that would have anchored the *Queen Mary* in a tempest. This was attached to oak after oak which were literally snatched up by the roots as easily as Jess deals with errant weeds which trespass in her flower beds. Within a few months, the park was a treeless, rolling desert, ready to be ditched and drained.

Perhaps you would have been among the many who threw up their hands in horror at such desecration? Grubbing up ancient trees could well be classed as a crime even more heinous than grubbing out ancient hedgerows. In considering crimes, it is useful to examine the motives for them, and there is no shadow of doubt that it would have been impossible to have farmed the land successfully without first removing the machine-shattering obstacles and then draining it

Whether the end justified the means in this case is a matter of subjective opinion. The park, by the end of the war, had a handful of trees which had once been famous but by then were as over-ripe as a crop of rotting fruit. They were all stag-headed and even the Beggar's Oak, despite all the cosmetic artistry of super-stitious guardians, had collapsed in mouldering ruins.

The remaining trees were survivors of a mass-felling by a thriftless owner in the 1930s who, so local rumour has it, dissipated 10,000 oaks for £10,000. They

LEFT The Walking Stick Oak is seventy feet to its lowest branch

The Beggar's Oak, spragged for generations of its decrepitude, eventually collapsed

Thistledown does not last so long

The Walking Stick was thunderstruck in 1906 and Jackson, the woodman, was told to decide whether to fell or spare it. He went with his brother, the goatherd who lived at Goat Lodge, and they decided to 'give it twelve months'. It still stands, eighty years later, though now it is dead – but no one will fell it for fear of bad luck

would now be worth more than the whole estate fetched in the sale, and all that survived was the unsaleable rubbish the timber merchant didn't bother to fell. What remained when the estate came under the hammer, therefore, was far from the magnificent timber which is mourned by all who are chronically alergic to change. The scenery reminded me of a painting of a Flanders battlefield, pock-marked by neglect instead of gunfire – but none the less ugly for that.

It is all too easy to believe that the countryside we initially remember was always like that so that any changes we see later appear to be the first changes which ever affected it. The fact is that the park above our wood had certainly been far more beautiful centuries ago when the ancient trees were in their prime. But ownership had passed to distant relatives for several generations so that there was no incentive to leave it better for successors. Each generation seems to have milked it before passing it on, not better but worse than when they inherited it.

The Walking Stick Oak still stands there on sufferance. The photograph shown was taken eighty years ago with the tree looking much the same as today, but with two stalwart countrymen symbolically propping it up. One of them was Jackson, the estate goatherd, who lived in our Lodge, and was responsible for the welfare of the historic herd of Bagot goats who destroyed more good timber than any hedge-grubbing farmer. The other, the goatherd's brother, was the woodman. Their occupations as the guardians of woodland and the goats which ravaged it were well-nigh incompatible.

Close scrutiny of the photograph shows a scar, spiralling down the Walking Stick trunk, caused by a bolt of thunder. I learned locally that the two men had been sent by the landowner to assess the lightning damage and decide if the tree was unsafe and must be felled or left in peace. They decided to leave it for a year to see if it became worse and then, a year later, they reprieved it. And there it still stands – and it is lucky, for the new owner who 'reclaimed' the park for agriculture was going to grub it out along with the other arboreal relics until he heard the tale of the curse of the Beggar's Oak. Deeming, I suppose, that discretion was the better part of valour, he left it where it was, though now it is dead and rotten as a hollow tooth. Perhaps he doesn't have it felled because he's wary of the beggar's curse – or perhaps because even tough millionaires sometimes have soft centres.

4. AS IT WAS

It took about a year to build an extension to the Lodge before we could move in, and since Brian Dale did not buy the farmland or wood until after that, Bagot's Park remained for some months the derelict feggy waste it must have been ever since the decent oaks had been felled in the 1930s. Curlew called and bred in the boggy tussocks, hares abounded, but the whole place was so plagued by poachers and foxes that the sporting rights on the whole 2000 acres fetched a rent of only £50 a year.

The Forestry Commission had already taken up their lease on the part of the wood where the standing timber had been sold when we bought the place. A timber merchant was hauling out the trunks as they were felled, and Fred Goodall from the nearby village was logging the 'lop-and-top' – that is, cutting up the sizeable branches and saplings, too small for the timber merchant, to be bagged and sold as firewood. The twigs and small branches were burned on huge bonfires to leave the whole site clear of brush and ready for the Commission to replant with their nasty little pine trees. Although there were a lot of trees, mostly oaks and birch in Holly Covert, there wasn't really much undergrowth for cover. For one thing, the shade from the top canopy of the mature trees shaded out the

built an extension which
concealed behind the
ginal cottage

understorey and, for another, the Bagot goats (*see* page 32) had played hell with anything that had the temerity to regenerate.

The understorey was several inches of peaty leaf-mould, accumulated over the centuries, and covered by a mat of bracken and feggy grass. Most seedlings, falling there, germinated and died before their roots could reach the peaty soil. The lucky ones that touched down on terra firma germinated but were peremptorily chopped off by the goats, ably assisted by the few rabbits that thrived there.

I found it astonishing – and very exciting – to discover that a few wild fallow deer still lay up in the concealment of bracken and low birch scrub which was all that had survived the vandal yowling of the chain-saws. With hindsight, I realise that they had been browsing the leaves of fallen trees that had previously been safely out of reach, and twenty-odd years spent actually *living* among wildlife, as opposed to catching fleeting glimpses on visits to the country, has taught me that mechanical noise and artificial light do not spell the same dangers to wildlife as they would to us.

Most exciting of all to us were occasional glimpses of badgers, foraging in the dusk of summer twilight or in the last hour before they went to ground at dawn.

I never take holidays now, because there is nowhere that I would rather be than here. However, when I was a cog in an industrial wheel, Jess and I used to stay at a fishing hotel in central Wales, in spite of the fact that rods and lines meant nothing to us. The attraction there was the scrubby oakwoods owned by the hotel; these woods were symphonies of nuthatch song, while the occasional cry of a curlew drifted down from the hills above. There were two badger setts which we crept out to watch after dinner until the light faded entirely but, above all, there was peace and tranquility – a world a million miles from the industrial rat-race where I earned my living.

At last we had escaped to what we hoped would be more solid values. We had managed to establish our territory where home would have all the attractions that our Welsh holidays had previously provided but for which I had had to suffer the treadmill for fifty weeks in order to enjoy the remaining two. As a practical writer, I hoped that my opportunities to recount, first hand, the facts I observed on my own patch would give me the edge over fellow scribes who were forced to rely on the experience of others. However much I may enjoy my life as a writer, success is still competitive!

I shall never forget the thrill of waking up in the knowledge that we owned a bit of England, even if it was neither valuable nor beautiful.

We arrived with no great altruistic notions about leaving the world better than we found it or with specific plans to conserve wildlife or create beautiful vistas. It was more than enough for us to have escaped from some of life's modern pressures. Instead of joining an ill-tempered scrum to work, through jostling traffic jams, it would be possible, henceforth, to tumble out of bed when daylight broke, to wander in our own woodland with the dogs, encouraging a grand appetite for a good breakfast. Henceforth, if deadlines did not press too hard, I could

The green woodpecker, which we know as the yaffle, finds food in the ancient trees

A few venerable oaks still bear witness to the ancient Forest of Needwood

leave my desk, no questions asked, at any time I liked, in order to chop logs, mow woodland rides or simply lean on gates in silent observation of fellow woodland dwellers. I wisely blotted out more pessimistic prospects – of there being no deadlines to press at all!

Jess and I went out with the dogs, two or three times most days, choosing a different direction each time. Even with a small wood like ours, it is surprising how long it takes to know it thoroughly. I had wandered through a stand of oak trees near the house literally hundreds of times before being surprised to find a carpet of little belly-aching apples beneath what I had always assumed to be yet another oak. It was, of course, a wild crab apple, forty or fifty feet high, with a trunk that my trouser belt would not have girthed. I felled a weedy ash and an ancient hawthorn, growing alongside, so that we could enjoy the prospect of the noble crab – and luxuriate with the logs from ash and thorn on winter fires. But it did drive home the early lesson that those who boast of knowing a wood like the back of their hand can easily be riding for a humiliating fall.

As a child I had been a great collector, which had originally sired my love of natural history. I had picked coltsfoot and buttercups, lady's smock and honeysuckle on the pitbanks near our house when I was young. In those days, 'collecting' was not rated as a vice, and toddlers took their trophies for display on their kindergarten nature tables. I was an inveterate collector of birds' eggs and butterflies, though the craze was so competitive that it was not done to tell schoolmates where to find such prizes, so far less damage was done than occurs when modern mindless louts vandalise trees and shrubs and any animal, bird or insect they can lay their hands on.

There were treasures in our wilderness at Goat Lodge that I had never recognised before. If I had seen tree-pipits on casual visits to other woods, I probably dismissed them from my mind along with all the other 'little brown jobs' which are often seen but are not all that easy to identify. But we had numerous tree-pipits in spring, silhouetted from the topmost twigs of the highest trees before climbing steeply skywards only to spiral down, like falling leaves, singing sweetly as they descended. There were grasshopper warblers, inconspicuous as shrews in the undergrowth, rasping messages of love so high pitched that my ageing ears can no longer hear them.

Neither bird had been present in my unsociable native pitbank habitat, and woodpeckers were rare. Green and greater spotted woodpeckers breed here regularly and we see lesser spotted, no bigger than starlings in the treetops, intermittently. It was all very exciting!

5. FULL CIRCLE

Sentimentalists wept bitter tears when the ancient park was cleared and drained and ploughed and sweetened with lime. They mourned the demise of the great oaks, however shaky and rotted by age; they wept crocodile tears when bracken, 'beautifully green in summer' and 'gorgeous with autumn tints', was engulfed by the plough; they even regretted the passing of the feggy grass which skinny goats on bare mountainsides would mock.

This part of central Staffordshire is undreamed of by outsiders. The ignorant believe that Staffordshire is costive with industry, from the Potteries in the north to the Black Country in the south. The fact is that this area is typical of many of the most beautiful parts of England. Central Staffordshire is a rich belt of undeveloped country, part woodland and part containing some of the finest dairy

g-headed oak on the edge of
paddock – a ghostly
ouette

fields in the land. It is an undiscovered oasis between the industrial deserts of the Potteries and the Black Country.

It had been kept inviolate for the simple reason that it consisted, until recently, of a few very large contiguous estates, where landowners would tolerate no intrusion. Instead of drunken English lanes lurching along the random boundaries between parishes, our lanes have been carved, straight as arrows, along the shortest distance between two points. This was possible because Needwood Forest covered the whole area and the route of a road was merely decided by the local landowner instead of being a tortuous compromise between parochial nabobs, so often too big for their boots. Such straight roads have wide verges, where cattle could graze on their last journey to market, and wildflowers bloomed to mark their passing.

In ancient times, the whole area had been indigenous hardwood forest which grew from seed and matured until it eventually rotted and collapsed without any help from man, leaving its own seedlings to regenerate and replace it. In medieval times, it was valued for hunting but clearings were made, first for settlements and then for farms. If modern preservationists had been around then, I expect they would have whinged about those first clearings cut for settlements. When more woodland was cleared for agriculture, they would as surely have been up in arms, as farmer-bashers are at any sign of change today.

Imagine, therefore, the hubbub when industry arrived – though nobody would have dreamed there had ever been anything but the benign tranquility of utter neglect when I first arrived here a quarter of a century ago.

The first hint I got was when the new owner's farm manager turned up with a lump of clay, covered with what appeared to be glazed china which had been criss-crossed with tiny cracks through having been placed in too hot a cooker. It was only the coincidence of having been involved in television programmes with craftsmen in the Black Country glass trade that sounded a chord of recognition. I had seen lumps of clay like that before, glazed with a coating of glass that had been crazed by tiny surface cracks, like plates left in ovens.

The hinterland of a deer park left unkempt and decaying for centuries is an unlikely place to find what looked like the broken lip of a crucible for melting glass – but the finder assured me there was plenty more where that came from. The huge machines that were being used for cutting the trenches for drains had unearthed it with the spoil – and there were also bricks among the rubble. These proved to be not the chunky rectangles that form the basis for modern housing estates but far slimmer, more elegant, handmade bricks that were used in the Middle Ages.

I took the chunk of glazed clay over to the cut-crystal glassworks we had televised and asked Colonel Williams-Thomas, the chairman, for his opinion. At first he was as puzzled as I was because, although he had no doubt that it *looked* like the lip of a clay crucible – or glass furnace – in his works, there was some indefinable difference he couldn't pinpoint.

We discovered later that there had been a medieval glass works in this part of Needwood Forest and what we had found was, indeed, part of a broken clay

Unspoiled country at the edge of Bagot's Wood – typical of this part of Staffordshire

Clue to the ancient glass-works

crucible, still coated on the inside with the glass which had been melted there.

Transport was so difficult in those days that it was easier to build a furnace near the source of fuel than it was to have a glass works to which fuel had to be carted. The fuel used was wood, so they built a furnace on the edge of a clearing and fed it from wood cut down nearby. When the furnace lining disintegrated, it was not rebuilt on the same site but as near as possible to the next patch of wood due for felling. When they 'reclaimed' the park as farmland, they found the remains of fourteen furnaces set approximately 400 yards apart.

The evidence showed that the oaks they used for fuel were not felled in the conventional sense but pollarded, by cutting off their branches, as is done with riverside willows. This would not only have involved less labour than felling by hand and then splitting trees of immense girth, but would have speeded up regeneration. When new branches grew, they would have been too high to be browsed by deer or goats which would have destroyed saplings as fast as they sprouted from seeds.

The far side of the park emerges onto a lane dividing the Park and Bagot's Wood from the Duchy lands, Marchington Woodlands, which are still part of the Crown lands belonging to Her Majesty the Queen. The lane drops down towards the nearest town, Uttoxeter, so sharply that, in times of storm, it runs with gooey clay giving it the name of Buttermilk Hill. This boundary of Bagot's Wood runs north-west from here, the Cliffs dropping down to fertile fields so steeply that they are barely economic to plant either as woods or fell, and they must look now much the same as they have looked for generations.

Consider the outcry there would have been, twenty years ago, if the new owner of the estate had wished to get planning permission for fourteen glassworks there! Yet the change was probably popular in medieval times. The contract was that two Huguenot refugees, who were master craftsmen, should make glass in Bagot's Park. The owner was to supply 'lodgings for the glassmakers and wood at the glasshouse door', in exchange for which the craftsmen made the glass and split the profits.

Surprising as the discovery of remains of what seemed to have been a thriving medieval glass industry may have been to us, reference to the one-inch Ordnance Survey map made us wise after the event. 'Glasshouse Bank' and 'Glass Farm' should have been broad enough hints to suggest that the landscape had not always been as it appeared on the surface.

Modern preservationists may scoff about such ancient, untamed parkland being prostituted for corn and beef, but if they bothered to trace the land's pedigree from Norman times, they would have found nothing but change. What had once been a hunting ground for kings had been consumed in the fires of glass furnaces; that dereliction had been landscaped into a picturesque amenity parkland which in turn had been desecrated by goats, sacrificed for sentiment as surely as by crystal entrepreneurs; and the relics left by taxation on feckless landowners were no better than a clapped-out battlefield in Flanders. But what is now misrepresented as a featureless factory farm is not managed half as heartlessly as modern farmer-bashers pretend.

6. HOLLY COVERT

Twenty-odd years soaking up the atmosphere here have taught me just how much one's values change. Holly Covert, the thirty acres of standing timber sold with a licence to fell, comes almost up to the back door of the Lodge. When I was trying to persuade the Australian-based estate owner to sell me the place, I explained to him that Holly Covert was the last few acres of the historic Bagot's Wood to escape the woodman's axe. If he would sell me Goat Lodge, the stone cottage originally built as an embellishment to the family's ancient deer park, I told him that this isolated stand of woodland would be left in peace as a memorial to what had once been a proud estate.

If the Lodge were sold with only the half-acre included in the agent's catalogue, the timber would be felled and sold, only to be replaced by the anonymous foreign softwoods that had condemned the rest of his family's heritage to undignified oblivion. As described earlier, my arguments appeared to convince him.

The crowns of fourteen of the oaks in the wood held the remnants of the ancient heronry which had enjoyed mixed fortunes down the generations. Before the war, the birds had built a mile or so to the north-west in Jordan's Croft and Buckley's Coppice. These were part of the 1000-acre Bagot's Wood; who Jordan and Buckley were seems to be a mystery, even to the indigenous local natives. All signs of any croft that could have been grazed by cattle have long since faded beneath a pall of trees.

Herons flying in to Holly Covert always tell us that spring is not far away

Holly Covert in spring

Heron-eye's view of Holly
Covert, Dunstal Pool and the
Lodge

But it had boded ill for the local herons when the oaks and other hardwoods were felled as a crop and the proceeds pouched by the landowner who then leased the land they'd grown on to the Forestry Commission for the next 999 years at an acorn rent. So although the ground was still owned by the family's heirs, it was but a nominal possession.

Such a vast area had not been felled in a season and dealers in standing timber are not a sentimental bunch. Three times in seven years, they had chopped down trees in which herons were actually nesting. Each subsequent season when the birds returned to breed as a colony and found their nests gone, they moved eastwards to the next stand of untouched timber and built their nests again, only to suffer the same fate as in previous years.

However, in the year that we arrived, they had moved across the drive to start a brand new heronry in Holly Covert. Although successive disasters had reduced their nests from forty-four to fourteen, pure luck had led them to our stewardship, which has guaranteed them continuous sanctuary ever since.

Herons are not a species seen every day. For one thing, their movements are seasonal and they congregate in heronries only in spring and summer to breed but disperse widely when their young are fledged.

Right from the start, we derived great pleasure from seeing them fly across the paddock daily – and went to their defence whenever they were threatened. Fishermen on the local reservoir accounted for some, and when I heard the bailiff telling his cronies in the local that he'd accounted for nineteen, I gave them an unwelcome squirt of publicity on the wireless. Water Boards are very thin-skinned

to adverse publicity so the unnecessary slaughter ceased and the number of herons' nests began a gradual but steady climb.

The first attraction of Holly Covert, therefore, was not the oak and birchwood there, though indigenous hardwoods are a shrinking asset in the countryside. The prime attraction was the heronry because the shy and beautiful birds personified the peace and tranquility for which we'd yearned so long in our years of urban life.

The other major attraction was the unique herd of Bagot goats. The legend which surrounds them is romantic. Their ancestors were reputed to have been used for milk and meat 'on the hoof' by the armies of King Richard I when he was fighting the infidels on his crusades. He was supposed to have brought them back with him and, in due course, the goats passed to his son, Richard II. One day, the king paid a regal visit to hunt in Needwood Forest which included the Bagot estate, and it is said that he was so pleased with the sport that he presented the goats to the Bagot of the day as a memento.

Some semblance of credibility is lent to the story because the Goat's Head crest was included in the Bagot coat of arms from Richard II's day. Why anyone who was grateful to his host should lumber him with anything as destructive as a goat is beyond my comprehension, but the herd certainly seems to have enjoyed the freedom of the estate for the next six centuries.

The assertion that goats will turn paradise into a desert is a gross understatement. If any shrub or tree has the temerity to regenerate, they nip it off at ground level. Mature oaks were ring-barked and stood naked and depressing as tombstones, while the odd tree that had just enough bark left to carry sap aloft stood there still in silent condemnation of the vandal goats.

The wood is marked Holly Covert on the map and documents from the last century record 'forest-sized holly trees, majestic in their mantle of Christmas snow'. By the time we arrived, all but two attenuated hollies had been ring-barked and decayed to litter on the forest floor. The 'Holly' in the covert was recalled by nothing better than a name on the map.

Practical commonsense decreed that the goats be banished, and it was soon obvious that the tenant farmers had done all in their power to put theory into practice for generations, because the goats had not only scrumped their crops but vandalised their hedges. My guess, although I never saw it happen, was that whenever the poor creatures ventured into view they found themselves on the wrong end of a charge of buckshot. Colour was lent to this theory because it was easier to creep up to the wild deer than to the famous herd of goats. And the first report of a gun in the distance panicked them into instant flight.

When the Forestry Commission leased the wood, in about 1949, they made it clear that the goats were no longer welcome there; the Commission's remit was to plant trees for growth, not goat fodder. And when Brian Dale bought the park to reclaim it for agriculture, he too wiped welcome off his sector of the map.

That left us, with our ninety acres of wood and pool and paddock, and I confess the goats found us a soft touch. They had the magic of centuries-old continuity in a shifting world where we and our like were clutching at the flimsiest straws of security.

What capped it for me was when, hearing a dog baying in the wood, I discovered a venerable billy goat, plastered in blood, standing in a circle of crimson snow fighting off a boxer dog which was attacking him. The courage and dignity of that old goat still haunts me. He and his ancestors had survived here, against all opposition, for 600 years. Who was I, an upstart interloper, to deprive them of their heritage?

For some years, therefore, the herd was sent up to the Big House which was open to the public, to be gawped at by trippers in the summer, and returned 'home' to the last bit of their ancestral woods for the winter and spring. The original animals had black heads, necks and legs, with white bodies, which made them look like black goats wearing white saddle cloths. The introduction of unrelated outsiders in the nineteenth century, supposedly to inject new blood, had resulted in coats of many mongrel colours. So I salved my reputation for unsentimental stockmanship by culling the mismarked specimens, gradually moulding the survivors to their traditional type and colours. I kidded the nannies in spring and returned them to their owner as an attraction to the paying public during the summer.

When the goats began to produce a dangerously high percentage of males, indicating virility was waning, they were passed to the Rare Breeds Survival Trust as a safeguard for their own survival.

So Holly Covert – and indeed the whole estate – is without the famous goats for the first time in more than six centuries. I have somewhat mixed feelings – but do not really regret their departure.

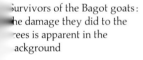

Survivors of the Bagot goats: the damage they did to the trees is apparent in the background

7. DAFFODIL LAWN

Daffodil Lawn is a long meadow of about six acres between Holly Covert and my boundary with the ancient deer park. When we came here, a decrepit oak fence divided us and, although there were gaps large enough for the passage of a bullock where palings had been pinched for firewood, it had once been a work of craftsman's art.

The estate workers had felled the oaks with axes and two-manned cross-cut saws, and the tree trunks had been cleft to size for palings with sledgehammers and steel wedges. The horizontal rails had been sawn in the estate timber yard, powered by a watermill which has since been submerged beneath the waters of Blithfield Reservoir, three miles away. Finally, the fence, which was five miles long, was erected by estate workers with enough faith to believe that it would stand as their memorial which future generations of their families could maintain with pride.

It is sad that such optimism has not been justified. An air of decadent gentility, which takes run-down estates and tumbledown buildings as its norm, wrings no tears of sympathy from me. Too many great estates have disintegrated for reasons ranging from sheer bad luck to idle incompetence, and from crippling death duties to slow horses and fast women. The decrepitude of that deer park fence was a sermon in wood that needed no words.

The northern side of Daffodil Lawn, between the pasture and the deer park fence, is bounded by a ditch which follows the gentle contours of the land to lead the eye to a delightful vista, one that owes nothing to the stark geometric patterns of conventional farming. Between this ditch and the fence beyond is a majestic belt of hardwood trees growing naturally where the seeds have fallen.

Wild daffodils

Across the drive, on my neighbour's land, the fence and wood and pasture continued in a larger meadow which the map described as Great Lawn. It had Lawn Coppice, a band of mixed hardwood, to the north, and Forestry Commission softwoods to the west and south. Such meadows were not created for commercial gain. They evolved from clearings in the forest to provide hay for the deer — and, in this case, goats — in winter, and rough grazing for the rest of the year. Holly Covert, hard by, had also been created not for ornament but use. Unappetising as the prickly leaves might be to us, deer and goats love them, so that the hollies were coppiced on rotation as fodder for the beasts.

We had first discovered Daffodil Lawn when we were prowling round the estate, trying to make up our minds whether or not to put in a bid at the sale for the cottage and adjacent woodland.

We were extremely concerned at the amount of poaching we saw going on. We surprised a man with gun and dog so often that we came to the conclusion that the gun was part of his anatomy. Legitimate game was so rare that the rent of £50 a year for sporting rights no longer seemed a pittance and the regularity with which we saw the same figures slide into the shadows suggested that they couldn't have come far and were probably locals. Such poaching had gradually

Signs of spring include the wild daffodils on the woodland lawn that took their name

been accepted as established custom because there hadn't been enough cash in the estate coffers to employ a keeper for years — and the landowners hadn't been interested in sport. As a result, the whole place was overrun by uninvited guests with guns who blazed away at anything that moved, from goats to deer to rabbits, wood pigeons and what few pheasants had survived. No type of poacher is worse because bringing one to book is a certain recipe for creating friction with neighbours who tend to unite against any disruptive stranger in their midst. The prospect of a war of attrition to gain control nearly put us off.

What tipped the scale, on the credit side, was the springtime carpet of little native daffodils which gave the meadow its attractive name of Daffodil Lawn. When we came over one sunny April afternoon, the delicate golden haze stole our hearts. Whether we could afford it or not, we determined to buy the place.

A week later, we brought close friends to share in our ambition and, we hoped, to bolster our confidence by encouraging us to escape to such a paradise. When we arrived on the scene, the daffs had gone! They hadn't reached their prime, flagged and formed seed heads. They hadn't been picked as poignant memories to soften the sadness of some local's passing, and they had not even been trampled or eaten by the deer or goats. Those dainty daffs had been deliberately shattered and torn to shreds by chain-harrows dragged over them by a tractor.

The chap who farmed the land had been plagued by trespassers who descended like swarms of locusts to pick the daffs, dig up the bulbs, trample the pasture and leave gates open for his cattle to stray as tokens of appreciation of their host's unwilling hospitality. So he destroyed the bait that lured them — and I have to admit that I sympathised with his aggravation!

The attractions of the ancient meadow were not bounded by wild daffs. To say the farming standard had been down to 'dog-and-stick' flattered it. There

The ancient deer fence which was our boundary when we came

were gaps in the fences through which grazing animals could stray at will, as they did through gates left open by trespassers. The grass was not cut for hay so that unpalatable tussocks were left to smother sweeter herbage that tried to sprout there, and ditches were not cleaned so that parts of the ground were puddled and swampy.

On the other hand, it was never sprayed with the poisonous chemicals which boost modern farming profits at the expense of all else; it wasn't doused with artificial fertiliser concocted to make grass grow – whatever else it smothers – and it hadn't been ploughed. Therefore, when the daffs were over or shattered by the harrows, 'weeds', including violets and cowslips, buttercups and daisies, took their place. There was wild honeysuckle and drifts of wood anemones under the trees and lady's smock and marsh marigolds in the boggy patches. Such unkempt, ancient meadows, where wild flowers can still thrive unblistered by farmers hooked on agrochemicals, are growing rare.

Our urge to escape from artificial city life was spurred on by the instinct to come to the defence of such places. If someone bought the land to squeeze the last New Penny profit by exploiting it, the result would surely be that the ancient turf would be ploughed and re-seeded with genetically pedigreed new leys which would spring skyward faster than Jack's beanstalk. The result would be that the cattle eating them would end up as utterly tasteless joints on supermarket shelves. Selective weedkillers would be sprayed to kill the 'weeds' that only thrived because they had enjoyed generations of toleration. Pesticides would annihilate the food of badgers and birds, and the shapely sickle of trees on the north side would probably be felled to make it easier to plough straight furrows.

The horrifically imagined perils to that meadow fired our determination to prevent such vandalism by leaving it as good as, or better than, we found it.

8. LORDS COPPICE

Our neck of the wood really is a neck in that the approximate square of ninety acres juts out from the east side of Bagot's Wood and is surrounded on the other three sides by farmland. The standing timber on the eastern half had been sold when we bought Goat Lodge so the timber merchant's men were hard at felling the biggest trees, lopping their branches off and taking the tree trunks or 'sticks' to their yard, twelve miles away. The mess such an operation makes on heavy clay, in a wet winter, is indescribable. The grassy woodland rides were first cut up and then ruts were gouged into watery channels a foot or eighteen inches deep. They were impassable to normal wheeled vehicles and even tractors, with metal tracks like tanks, floundered to a halt on their bellies until branches were dropped in to provide a temporary hard bottom.

Noble trees that had surveyed the scene for centuries crashed into the mud, mocking our impotence to do anything about it. When we had first seen the standing trees, before we had actually bought the place, they had promised endless seasons of pleasure as we got to know the birds and beasts which would share them with us. Although we knew, in theory, that the standing timber had been sold and would be felled in that part of the wood, it hadn't dawned on us just how obscenely naked they would leave the ground when they were gone.

The man who bought the trees contracted to leave the land clear and ready to be replanted by the Forestry Commission. But small crooked trunks, branches, twigs and leaves are no good to timber merchants so Fred Goodall was called in.

The rides were pitted and
rutted by the timber fellers

Looking across the paddock, over the pool and the deer glade: Lords Coppice is on the right

My first meeting with Fred and his mate Bill will remain a vivid memory long after the more recent past has faded. There was never much doubt about where they were working because they had a huge portable circular saw mounted on a tractor, and the menacing whine, as it reduced great branches to logs, was audible half a mile away.

The day after we bought the place, I followed the sound of the saw and homed in on them at the southern corner of Lords Coppice. Fred was some way away, reducing great branches with a chain-saw to a size he could lift. Not knowing which was the gaffer, I went up to Bill who was cutting branches to logs on the circular saw.

He took no notice as I drew near but the saw revolved at such high speed that the din was ear-splitting so I assumed he hadn't noticed my approach. I waited until he'd finished a branch and then passed the time of day to which he replied as courteously as countryfolk do, though he didn't appear to look at me. When I asked how long they would take to finish, he said I'd better ask Fred, for he was the gaffer. He jerked his thumb in the direction of the yowling chain-saw and started sawing logs again as if I weren't there.

Fred proved to be a delightful countryman who made his living following the timber fellers, burning the brash or unsaleable rubbish and converting good lop-and-top into wood for his log round. He explained that Bill helped him, but not to take much notice if he seemed a bit offhand. He wasn't rude, he said. It was just that he was blind.

The idea of a blind man cutting logs on an unguarded circular saw gripped the pit of my stomach. It was so preposterous that I did not, at first, believe it and returned to have another word with Bill to check if my leg was being pulled. He might have been able to tell light from dark, but had to locate each branch with the toe of his boot and the precise position of the spinning saw roughly by sound and exactly by feeling for the edge of the sawbench.

Such risks would be out of the question now because the Health and Safety man would blow his gasket. But twenty years ago, nobody seemed to bother; Bill was happy to have some variety in his sightless world and Fred derived satisfaction because he was the only chap in the village who would put himself out to ease the monotony of the young man's life. But, whatever it did for Bill, the operation ruined the outlook in our wood.

The timber merchant winched the huge trunks on wire hawsers over the ground to the great timber-drug, on which they were piled precariously, to be dragged along the rutted woodland rides to the relatively hard surfaced drive which passed the Lodge. Ground so desecrated soon resembled a shell-torn battlefield which was not improved by Fred's tractor following the drug with trailer-loads of logs. Half the woodland paradise to which we were escaping was being transformed to ashes before we settled in. But at least they were *our* ashes, for now we really owned our bit of England and, whenever we went round the land, we were often pleasantly surprised.

In autumn, the wood is redolent with the powerful stench of stinkhorn fungus

The first spring after the south-eastern half of the wood was felled, there was a stubbly beard of small birch undergrowth, amongst which weakly bramble patches thickened and spread as if by magic. That summer, quite a few grasshopper warblers nested there — and I had neither seen nor heard the species before. They are dainty and small, and they skulked in patches of thick cover left unspoiled by either the felling or the lop-and-topping. We didn't notice them at first, assuming that their song was not the sound of birds but of the grasshoppers which gave them their name for strident warbling. It is an almost continuous, high-pitched stridulation, far less undulating than the rasping produced by the hind legs of conventional grasshoppers. Jess and I used to go up there in the evenings and perch comfortably on the stump of one of the trees we mourned, while the grasshopper warblers rasped out their lamenting dirge.

From time to time, we saw one emerge from the safety of his cover, a small dull brown bird, creeping through the undergrowth as stealthily as a mouse. And, as a bonus, when dusk was falling, his high-pitched, rapid notes were sometimes merged with the more musical, louder churring of a nightjar (*see* page 69). Neither bird was familiar to us — and formerly we would cheerfully have journeyed hundreds of miles on holiday to hear them. So, however derelict and battle-scarred Lords Coppice looked, it was irresistible to us, and we revelled in its solitude.

We hear neither bird there now because the land was planted with horrid, sterile pines which prospered at the expense of almost all else, choking and shading out the undergrowth which had once attracted the grasshopper warblers and nightjars.

We made up our minds that, by hook or by crook, we would reverse the process.

9. PRIMROSE DELL

The eastern tip of Ley Close is labelled Marl Pit on the map, but it is Primrose Dell to those who know it. When we came, it was a small pool, about twenty yards by thirty, fed by natural drainage from the wood. Its official name tells us that the hollow was man-made, with hundreds and hundreds of tons of sticky clay being dug out with pickaxe and spade by our industrious forebears. The marly clay was rich in carbonate of lime so it was taken all over the farms, by horse and cart, and spread on the land to sweeten it.

But the pool was fed by natural drainage over the acidic bracken and oak peat of the wood and, when a specialist from the River Board tested the water, he said it would be 'just right for topping up car batteries'! Something of academic licence, perhaps, but it did have a pH value of 4·5.

It was the profusion of primroses, in spring, which really stole our hearts. The banks above the pool had clumps as big as buckets of the truest yellow purity. Some of the clumps were so ancient that they had spread until they merged

The prosaic 'marlpit' on the map proved to be the delightful pool at Primrose Dell

with next-door neighbours, and there were sprays of cowslips, too, which had interbred occasionally to produce a smattering of oxlips. Delicate violets and golden marsh marigolds were additional delights, while dog's mercury and giant marestail spoke as authentically of ancient lineage as the pedigrees vouched for by Debrett link noble families with antiquity.

The giant marestail was particularly fine but it thrives best in ancient forest and its presence in our wood traced its origin back to Needwood Forest before clearings were cut for settlements – and long, long before the medieval glass industry coppiced oaks for smelting glass.

One evening, Jess and I sat on a tree trunk, high above the pool, and looked over to Squitch Bank where cattle were turned out for a few shillings a head, to get what nourishment they could from the feggy pack-belly that masqueraded as 'summer grazing'. We'd been sitting motionless and quiet for perhaps half an hour, when a tiny pinprick of light in the centre of a clump of rushes caught my eye. I gave no indication that I had seen it, but froze, moving only my eyes to establish the source of the reflected light. I was soon rewarded when it flashed again. It turned out to be a fox, curled in his rushy couch as comfortable as a lapdog on a cushion. He must have been there when we arrived and, realising we hadn't spotted him, though no more than twenty yards away across the water, he had calculated camouflaged immobility was safer than flight. The flashing jewel which had caught my attention was simply sunshine mirrored in his amber eye.

I murmured to Jess, to alert her of his presence, but though she never moved a muscle – except her own eyes to watch him – he must have sensed that we knew he was there and was gone in a flash.

The depth of tranquility that allows observers to merge with their surroundings, sitting so long without sight or sound of other people, was exactly what we had hoped for when we had shaken the dust of industry off our feet. The peace in Primrose Dell was the perfect therapy after a score of back-stabbing years in the competitive world of commerce. No need for sharp city suits here, for there was nobody else to see them. A crumpled jacket and corduroys, open-necked shirt and tough wellies were good enough for us. The sheer luxury of being able to tumble out of bed to wander wherever we liked in whatever clothes were most comfortable is the stuff that escapist dreams are made of. Even if the price we had to pay was hard physical labour in all weathers, the attraction of living creatures, whether farm stock or wildlife, were irresistible, at least in theory!

The seclusion of our wood, however temporary, and the delights of watching wildlife, however uncomfortable the weather may be, are worth almost any price – but the party was too soon over.

As soon as Fred and his blind mate had flogged the saleable logs and put the rest on their bonfire, the Forestry Commission workers moved in. They arrived with wedge-shaped planting spades and transparent plastic bags stuffed to the brim with little pine trees, each about a foot in height.

Each worker filled a bag with little trees, slung it around his waist and, with the other planters strung out across the open space, he set off in a predetermined line. Every four feet, he paused momentarily to stamp on his spade to cut a slit

Primrose Dell greets spring
with primroses and marsh
marigolds, and remembers the
past with the primitive giant
marestail

in the virgin woodland soil and then thrust the roots of a treelet into the ground; another stamp closed the jaws of the slit onto the tender roots, and the planter moved on another four feet to repeat the operation. When the line of planters had gone, they left behind them stereotyped rows of treelets, four feet apart in the row and five feet, cross-country, to the next row.

This didn't seem too bad across the desert of tree stumps where ancient trees had been felled and Fred and Co. had burned the lop-and-top. At least it was restoring some order out of chaos, even if the order consisted of identical rows of sterile foreign pines.

It was rather different on the flowery turf round Primrose Dell where it was obvious that the most beautiful traditional flowers of the English countryside were about to be sacrificed for get-rich-quick commercial softwoods.

Every evening after the forestry workers had knocked off and gone home, Jess and I walked round to see what they had done to our beloved wilderness, for the last thing we wanted was to have it 'restored' to the order of boring, evergreen uniformity. There was, however, nothing we could do about it — legally. The tenancy agreement made by our predecessors stipulated that the tenants could replant the felled area with any trees they liked — and softwoods offered the quickest return.

But I was brought up with a bunch of poaching colliers who are not the easiest chaps for bureaucrats to push around, and I have been used to running my own affairs.

The seedling trees arrived in transparent plastic sacks which were left in heaps overnight, to be planted by the foresters each day. So each evening, we pulled up any trees planted round Primrose Dell that day, and returned them to the sacks of trees waiting to be planted. The following day, the workers took them out and patiently planted them again. I suspect that each knew what game the other was playing, but we greeted each other with poker-faced politeness, as if nothing was amiss.

It could have continued for ever, but their stakes were money and ours were love. Love won, for they submitted first, leaving the primrose patch round the dell unplanted. It gave us hope for the future.

Tick, my pointer, and me, with Forestry Commission trees behind

10. BLUEBELLS AND BRACKEN

Ley Close runs from Lords Coppice, along the east side of the wood, to the hillock that dips to Primrose Dell. It is an extraordinary bit of country, bounded on the east by a hedge of blackthorn and whitethorn mixed, belonging to a neighbour who insists on keeping it barbered by a foul modern mechanical hedge-cutter. The only shade it casts on his pasture is from the weakly setting sun, so the profits from his outlay seem to benefit nothing but the precision of an ultra-tidy mind. Left to rampage on its own wayward course, the hedge would thicken into ideal cover for scores of pairs of nesting birds.

The one advantage to us is that we get a superb unobstructed view across the valley to three farms over the other side. They are isolated farms, served by a dead-end lane from the village a couple of miles away and, beyond them, the main road to Burton is another mile, as the crow flies. The spacious, well-wooded view across some of the best dairying country in the land gives a satisfying sense of solitude, feeding once more the deep nostalgia to escape from the empty rush of modern life.

On our side of the hedge, in Ley Close, the original hardwood timber had been exposed to harsh east winds which had stunted it and then the goats had annihilated most of the hazel bushes and small trees. Bracken, which is almost indestructible, had taken over and run riot.

Many casual visitors to the countryside love bracken. They say that its bronze autumnal tints are worth a king's ransom and that its green fronds, in late spring and early summer, take their breath away. For my part, I hate the stuff. It is poisonous so that deer and stock won't eat it, and even rabbits leave it alone. And it grows so thickly that its fronds make a canopy as dense as sterile pines, so that nothing thrives beneath it. The one exception seems to be bluebells which sprout and flower before the season's crop of bracken matures.

Ley Close puts on an annual show of both. When we wandered, exploring, round the wood, we were captivated by the blue haze of bluebells in late spring, for here was a bluebell wood that went back to antiquity.

When the chaps from the Forestry Commission turned up to plant their miserable little trees, every four feet, in rows five feet apart, we writhed in agony for the fate of the delicate bulbs. But it was one thing to secrete a few hundred trees back in the bags they came in, to prevent the desecration of Primrose Dell, and quite another over a wide area like Ley Close. Even friendly foresters would have taken umbrage at that!

We needn't have bothered. They planted their trees – and the bracken writhed up and threatened to choke them. The men came with sickles and slashing hooks and started their endless, backbreaking chore, up one row and down the next, cutting down the bracken to give the young trees light and air.

The bluebells joined in the game. For centuries they had survived and achieved a balance with the bracken by growing and flowering before the bracken grew high enough to smother them from view. With foresters as their unlikely allies,

A thick carpet of bluebells — one of the most marvellous sights of spring

Bracken is a favourite couch for does to drop their fawns

they relished the additional light and air that resulted from the bracken's temporary demise. The bluebells thickened to a mat — and the slashed bracken sprouted and grew again so that the little pines had no chance of getting so much as a hair-root into the door of this new territory.

So there are several acres up on the top of Ley Close that must look much as they looked before the woodmen came. There is an ancient hedge maple, a few hawthorns, some wild rose, odd alders and hazels, and a carpet first of bluebells and then of bracken, dotted with what few pines survived the combined attacks, not of nature-loving man but of man-assisted nature.

Visitors love it because it is a microcosm of what they dream was the ancient wilderness before we interfered by changing everything. Nothing could contrast

more vividly with today's centrally-heated, automated, pressurised modern life.

I beg to differ. The struggle for survival and territory between those immigrant trees and the native bluebells and bracken is as bitter as anything that goes on among the rival factions in our inner cities. The main difference is that, up on Ley Close, the pace is the slowest of ultra-slow slow-motion. The bracken has its uses as nesting cover for pheasants, for deer to drop their fawns into and for the odd woodcock to skulk under. But it provides virtually no food and it is as lethal as mass-produced pine trees for preventing regeneration of young native trees or the survival of most flowers.

Bluebells are among the few exceptions that seem able to co-exist with bracken, for they are equally invasive. Indeed, Jess would say they are far worse because the odd bulbil gets into her garden with the leaf-mould we cart from the wood. Before she has time to sneeze, there are bluebells in every border, first competing with her cossetted flowers and then annihilating them as the bracken does the little trees. And once bluebells establish themselves among garden flowers, they are the very devil to weed out. A carpet of them is a wonderful sight – on someone else's land!

Quite by accident, I stumbled across a craftsman-built brick culvert, right in the middle of a dense patch of bracken, high up on Ley Close. It was beautifully constructed, of handmade wedge-shaped bricks which fitted into a perfect horse-shoe, so that the greater the weight, at the crown of the arch, the tighter they jammed together to support it. The culvert was only about twelve feet long, and was now below ground level because generations of bracken peat had been deposited on it as season after season's bracken and bluebells had died and withered to dust. I shouldn't have found it at all if some animal had not excavated quite large tunnels to the entrance and exit.

It was puzzling, at first, to decide why it had been built where it was, because the ground round about was fairly level, but it was apparent that the large tunnels to the entrance had been dug by badgers and there was evidence of leaves and bracken fronds being dragged in and out as bedding. Badger latrines close by, with fresh dung in them, confirmed the diagnosis.

As time went on, I discovered several similar culverts spread, apparently haphazardly, through the wood, harking back to the days when the estate had been well run, when the estate workers had used slack seasons to put ditches through the wood and to cross them with woodland rides supported by these superbly constructed brick culverts. Most of the ditches had been filled to the brim with autumn leaves which had rotted over the years to peaty soil, which in turn supported a mat of vegetation consigning the ditches to oblivion.

Wildlife does not forget so easily because such sanctuaries are scarce and invaluable. The ditches were blocked and backed up with water in wet seasons, flooding the floor of the culverts and making them untenable, so they were vacant in winter. But as summer approached, they dried out in time to make snug bachelor flats for testy old boar badgers who were finding boisterous cubs in larger setts a nuisance. So I look the culverts over about once a week in fine weather because it is as good as a formal roll-call of the current badger population.

Ancient craftsmen built brick culverts under woodland rides; they run with water in winter but harbour badgers when the warm weather dries them out

11. DUNSTAL POOL

It seemed incomprehensible that anyone, even in days of very cheap labour, should bother to dig a ditch through ancient forest which had grown where God had dropped the seed instead of being planted with geometric uniformity solely for profit.

In front of the Lodge, less than a hundred yards across the paddock, is Dunstal Pool. It covers an acre and a half and has 'naturally' curving banks on three sides, and a bank built as a straight dam on the fourth.

When we bought it, we discovered this fourth side was indeed a dam, constructed in years gone by to back up the water and form a reservoir, with a minimum of labour, to supply two of the estate farms further down the valley. A pool is no good as a water supply if it does not have a constant supply of water to replenish it, which explained the presence of the main ditch, almost half a mile long, threading its way through Holly Covert.

It is a ditch and a half because, standing in the bottom, my eyes don't reach high enough to peer over the bank, and its sloping sides are about ten feet apart at ground level.

Wild duck keep safe from foxes by constantly swimming to keep the water free from ice

When I see a ploughman take his tractor into a hundred-acre field, I often think that the prospect of going up and down the furrows until what must look like an endless desert is ploughed would drive me round the bend. How much more daunting must it have been for labourers to dig themselves eye-deep into the ground in the wood above Dunstal Pool, knowing that they were destined to dig and shovel and pickaxe their way for half a mile through the roots of an ancient forest. Their faith in the future must have been deeper than mine.

I have walked every foot of that ditch, cleared out minor debris which had fallen in over the years, and soon after we came I ejected some local trespassing lads who were damming it to make themselves a private swimming pool. Before they went, I made them dig out what they had chucked in, from which experiment they discovered it is easier to shovel soil down into a pit than to pitch it up again.

The muscular civil-engineering feat of digging such a ditch from our pool to eternity would have been futile if there had been no water to trickle in at the other end and, sure enough, I found a spot on the Ordnance map, at the north-west corner of Daffodil Lawn, clearly marked 'Spring'. It was at the junction where the north side of the lawn joins the park and the west side joins the drive which passes our house to service the farm beyond. The rest of the estate had not yet been sold and, as this would be the only possible water supply to our meadow, I asked our lawyer to make sure that the deeds showed that the spring was within our boundary.

Although Dunstal Pool was so close to the house, it was of no great advantage originally because very little of it was visible due to of a fringe of birch scrub which covered a peninsula on the far side, and a mass of rank rushes on our side.

On an occasion when we had hired a JCB digger to level an area for the foundations of the extension to the house, I asked the driver to cross the paddock and 'doze' out the offending intervening rushes. To our astonishment, we discovered that this side of the pool had such a hard bottom, of large pebbles and impacted clay, that the great machine could be driven into the water to cavort about in the shallows and simply scoop away the rushes, roots and all, to leave the view from the house unimpaired.

The only rarity was bogbean, but rarity does not have top priority with me and when Canada geese scoffed it one year (*see* page 89) I shed no tears over its passing. I'd rather see the ever-changing patterns of flighting wildfowl from the window than know an obscure rarity is skulking, unseen, at water level.

Clearing the near bank, however, made limited vision over the peninsula even more infuriating. The goats had roamed round the pool for years and ring-barked all the smaller trees with the sweetest bark. Small birch, with rough, gnarled bark, were left, as were oaks too big for successful stripping. But the twiggy labyrinth that was left produced the infuriating sensation of peering, in vain, for dramas enacted behind lace curtains.

Several species of wildfowl flighted in at dusk, and we had endless hours of pleasure watching them. The ripples on a pool are caused by air movement, either

The wild duck flight into
Tunstal Pool at dusk – our
favourite time

wind or warm air rising or cold air sinking as temperatures change when the sun sets or rises. There are a few magic minutes most evenings when the air temperature drops so that the cooling air sinks like an eiderdown, smoothing every ripple on the water surface until it is becalmed, and as bright and motionless as a mirror.

It so happens that this utter calm and stillness usually coincides with the setting sun whose horizontal rays turn common looking-glass to a priceless golden mirror. To make perfection even more perfect, this is the time the wild duck choose to arrive. They come in groups of two or three, skimming down to shatter the still surface into droplets of gold. And before calm settles they often flight off again, chasing each other in playful circles before returning, sometimes accompanied by several more wild friends and relatives.

No kaleidoscope ever displayed more varied, exciting patterns, and on summer evenings we sat enthralled watching *our* wild duck visiting *our* pool and putting on displays of jewelled aerobatics that once we would cheerfully have saved up for a year to see. The risks and traumas of chucking up a safe job in industry were more than worth it for the sheer delights of watching this one corner of our wilderness for the few magical minutes of sunset.

12. LUCK OR LUNACY

Although the ambition to quit the world of ruthless commerce is almost universal among my friends, few put it into practice and regard decisions to do so either as luck or lunacy, depending on whether they succeed or fail.

The first yardstick of our success was the view across the paddock from our sitting-room window and first impressions were definitely on the side of lunacy. This was because the most optimistic visionary would never have described the expanse of churned-up mud dipping down to Dunstal Pool as 'paddocks'.

One side was bounded by knee-deep ruts — or 'rits' as the locals call them — which had been gouged out of the cloying clay by the caterpillar tracks of the crawler tractor which dragged the tree trunks to the timber merchant's 'drug', or wagon. The extent of this morass was exaggerated by the desecration left when the hedge which had run from the cottage to the pool had been grubbed out. The place resembled a battlefield the day after the troops had pulled out.

So Fred came to the rescue once more, as he has so often done since — and I am glad to say, still does. He turned up with an old-fashioned fiddle drill, a relic of days when farming was more of an art than a science. Fred had inherited the skills of his forebears, so it gave me more pleasure to watch him displaying the mastery of his craft than I should have derived from any maestro coaxing melody from his conventional violin.

Spring brought confirmation that Nature approved as much as I did because the barren muddy patch blossomed into an even green paddock to the edge of the wood, and could not fail to fill one's eyes with pleasure.

I was able to chronicle the resurrection and turn an honest penny by beginning a weekly column, called 'Goat Lodge Diary', for the *Birmingham Evening Mail* which, under various titles, has continued ever since. If I couldn't make a living by farming the land or selling the timber, it was encouraging to discover that others were prepared to pay for the privilege of sharing the experience, if only at second hand.

I had surrounded the garden and pool at the Cottage with wire netting in order to keep a variety of pinioned wildfowl from straying and, by fixing an electric fence high up the netting, powered by a waterwheel, I had rendered it reasonably fox- and cat-proof.

We also kept a wonderfully tame female roe deer which I had hand-reared on the bottle so we naturally brought her and the wildfowl with us to Goat Lodge. If we had simply turned them loose, the foxes would have raided the waterfowl, and the deer, never having learned the need to mistrust mankind, would have been nobbled as quickly by the predatory men with guns who infested the place when we came.

So we fenced in a corner of the pool and the paddock and house and garden. Jess said it was tantamount to being imprisoned, but its purpose was to fence intruders out rather than to incarcerate the inhabitants.

The other great advantage was that we could give the dogs the freedom of the enclosure, including the back door of the house, the garage, tractor shed and outbuildings where the domestic poultry roosted. Tough, the Alsatian, was bred at police kennels and soon acquired a formidable reputation for never stopping barking until she'd got a mouthful. As this is an isolated spot – and I enjoy training dogs – I have taken the trouble to keep dogs which follow the same tradition, and he would be a stupid intruder who faced my present Alsatian, Belle, or Tarka my Rottweiler, uninvited and unchaperoned. I put more faith in hard-mouthed guard dogs than electronic wizardry to deter or detect prospective burglars.

he fiddle drill is a simple seed
ontainer, with straps to
spend it from the sower's
oulders. A large horizontal
ox positions the seed, and a
osely woven bag attached to
ensures that a load can be
rried about twice the capacity
the box. A hole in the
ottom of the box can be
ntrolled to the right diameter
allow seed to trickle through
any predetermined rate. The
d drops onto a finned
eader which is spun back
d forth by a 'fiddle' bow that
ve the contraption its name.
e faster the bow oscillates,
faster spins the spreader to
an even arc of seed. By
sting the aperture size, the
trol of seed, and the stroke
he fiddle bow to spin the
ader, it is possible to sow
st any desired
centration of seed

13. INSTANT GARDEN

Jess is a mad keen gardener and before we came to Goat Lodge, she had spent the previous seven years slaving to re-create the garden at our last house which had fallen into decay when we bought it. The Cottage had been a glorious place once and still had great potential. A strong stream, from the mill across the road in the village, fed two pools with a waterfall under the bedroom window; a natural lullaby. When we arrived, the pools were silted up and the stream diverted outside our boundary, so cleaning them out and repairing the water input was a labour of love.

Neglected jungles of rhododendrons and azaleas, planted in the Victorian era, were cleared and disciplined back to encourage their gorgeous springtime colours. To round things off, there was a rookery of about fourteen nests in the great lime trees across the drive, and this contributed a perfect duet with the waterfall on peaceful summer mornings.

The Cottage itself had once been a yeoman's half-timbered farmhouse which looked lovely and was comfortable – however much it drained resources with insatiable demands for repairs, from roof to damp foundations! Small wonder, then, after so much effort, that Jess was reluctant to swap it for a derelict cottage with a derelict wood – and no garden at all!

The summer nights are scented with honeysuckle

The Cottage garden was mature, with rhododendrons and flowering shrubs

There had once been an orchard at Goat Lodge, but the goats had got in and ring-barked the fruit trees to leave nothing but brambles and rotting dereliction. When they had finished masticating the orchard, they killed the holly hedge that once provided privacy as one walked from the back door, through the jungle of nettles that clothed the yard, to the two-seater earth closet next to the pump. The other side of the house was a thicket of hawthorn and bramble scrub, too tough even for the goats to tackle.

I got nowhere by telling Jess how lucky she was that the whole place was a shambles because we could never have afforded what it would have fetched in prime condition. She preferred the patch she had restored with love and hard labour to starting again from scratch.

The chap who bought the Cottage planned to build modern little boxes upon the paddock (and his successors even filled the pool to provide another 'desirable plot'!) so he didn't care what happened to the garden, and gave us permission to take anything we wanted with us.

Jess was mollified and I have described in *My Beloved Wilderness* how at Goat Lodge we bulldozed the scrub and paddocked a bunch of pigs there to clear the weeds, muck it and leave the tilth perfect for planting. A couple of days' hire of a landscape gardener, his gang of labourers and a lorry for transport produced an instant garden, to Jess's design, with all her cosseted shrubs planted just where she wanted them. It would have taken a fortune to buy them in their

ess created her garden at the odge on the foundation stock e transplanted from the ottage

mature and perfect state, or half a lifetime to grow them from the size supplied by nurserymen.

But 'instant' garden is really a misnomer. Gardens never stand still for they are always improving or dying back, becoming overgrown or sparse. Jess, therefore, has spent the intervening years of hard labour striving to make the garden even more perfect. However tired she is, she claims to gain solace and relaxation

We brought a tiny yew hedge from the Cottage and planted it to conceal our new extension once it had grown

A few years later, there were signs that our plan to split old from new by a dense yew hedge would work

just sieving her green fingers through the fertile soil. The day she said she liked it as well as the last was a highlight to remember.

It is a practical garden, with a hornbeam hedge along two sides, and a yew hedge from the drive to the house. This yew hedge was only two feet high when we brought it from the Cottage and we expected it to be very slow growing. But the chaps who transplanted it did a good job, double-trenching and making a base of peat and rich soil to take the transplants. The object of the exercise is for it to grow so tall that it isn't possible to see much of the old house from the side of the new extension – and nothing of the new when admiring the original lodge from the front garden.

Inside the hornbeam hedge is a hedge of rhododendrons, for privacy from the drive and as a windbreak. And, on the pool side of the garden, clumps of bamboo blunt the spite of searching east winds – and provide the perfect nesting cover for canbottles, or long-tailed tits.

The kitchen garden is on the other side of the main garden, nearer the pool – but our neighbours have a farm shop and Gordon is a good greengrocer in the local market town. So we concentrate on strawberries and raspberries, peas and kidney beans, and spinach and onions, leeks and herbs. We both love sharp cheese and pickled onions, and I love a couple of huge onions boiled with a trotter from one of the pigs we fatten on acorns in the wood. We don't bother with spuds and cabbage or sprouts or cauliflower, apart from the odd row to be picked fresh in emergency. I say 'we' don't bother, but whereas I don't mind digging out a rabbit when I'm ferreting, I have no stomach at all for gardening. Help from the village half a day a week suffices to fill the gaps.

Jess does the flower borders with the help of young Ruth Springthorpe, without whom the whole place would stop. She is the daughter of Gerald and Ann, old family friends, and we regard her as a member of the family.

Although the so-called simple transfer of Jess's beloved flowering shrubs from the Cottage provided the basis, additions of new flowers and shrubs and heathers and oddities to attract butterflies and birds appear, as if by magic, every time she and Ruth pass (or fail to negotiate!) a garden centre or nursery.

The wire-netting fence I put up originally to keep out the deer was soon replaced by a less obtrusive ha-ha; honeysuckle and wisteria take the starkness from the walls of the house, the huge slab of stone that was the Lodge's original larder step is a link with the past as a piles-producing seat at the far end of the lawn, and gentle curves lead to mysteries beyond immediate view.

It isn't a large garden and the grass on the lawns would be sprayed as a weed by bowling-green keepers. But every flower in every bed has personal associations that fill Jess's eyes with nostalgic pleasure. She remembers one flower as a link with a fellow garden lover in Hereford, a certain shrub spells a memorable day out somewhere else, and a herb recalls the visit of a deeply-respected radio producer. This snippet arrived with a bread-and-butter letter from one dear friend, and that reminds her of a visit to another. The whole garden is quiet, peaceful and colourful – and Jess feels more rested while working there than relaxing anywhere else.

14. 'CONTROL' BADGERS

I have described in detail in previous books how I found badgers, which lived in setts on my neighbour's land, feeding in my wood. The reason seemed to be a matter of convenience because our land is cold, soggy clay, which would be most uncomfortable to excavate, while over the boundary the soil changes to well-drained, sandy gravel which is easy to dig and is warm and dry to sleep in, so the badgers came to the wood only to feed.

In order to encourage the badgers, I built an artificial earth in the bank above Dunstal Pool but was so ignorant about the techniques of ventilation that the result was mouldy and mildewed and the local badgers turned up their snouts at it (*see page 114*). Unaware of the reason, I conceded defeat and, as described in *Badgers at My Window*, I hand-reared three cubs which I eventually established at liberty to come and go as they liked.

Bill Brock, my hand-reared badger, ran free in the wood but still came through the window to pay his nightly respects

ared a pair of sow cubs to
p Bill company

The badgers settled in an artificial sett I built within view of the sitting-room window

To the entrance of the artificial sett I had built for them at the edge of the wood opposite the sitting-room window, I fitted a device to monitor their comings and goings and punch up the times on a barograph in my study. This was bastardised from a redundant barograph I bought as scrap off an obsolete heat treatment furnace, sold as bankrupt stock. It was adapted by a methods engineer I knew when I was in industry and, although a bit Heath Robinson by modern standards, it did the job I wanted.

Each time a badger left or entered the artificial sett, my old contraption punched up the time on the barograph, and for five long years of this relentless clocking in and out the badgers themselves recorded with split-second precision their exact periods of activity and rest at the sett.

Academic scientists record different things but I have to confess I was sceptical of the chap who once stated in a lecture to his fellow boffins that badger-watching was easy for him since he knew, to within ten minutes, the time when the animals would oblige by coming out to be observed. To give authenticity to the story, he said he had confirmed his results by watching badgers on several hundred occasions.

The records on my barograph – which covered all night, not just the hours of twilight – clocked up more than 2000 consecutive nights during those five years. Times of emergence and re-entry varied unpredictably, having little obvious relation to daylight, weather, temperature or season. All my experiment taught me was that badger behaviour was among those mysteries of life which are still beyond our ken.

Jess and I derived endless pleasure from our badgers. The purists may scoff about being anthropomorphic if one treats animals as being highly intelligent creatures which are far from being the reflex-impelled automatons science says they are. Even after more than five years' continuous observation, I was no nearer to unravelling the intricacies of badger behaviour than when I started.

One thing I did learn is that badgers are not slaves of reflex impulse but individuals in their own right. Some are aggressive, others relatively gentle. There are idle and industrious badgers, sows which are perfect mums, and grumpy creatures which drive off the cubs to seek fresh territory as soon as they are self supporting, however inhospitable the surroundings.

Some scientists will argue that it is all due to population pressure, local food supply, human or other disturbance and a whole gamut of theories which can neither be proved nor disproved. Although I do not pretend to know the answers, it does not inhibit my pleasure of sharing the wood with a whole variety of creatures whose ancestors were probably hereabouts long before my forebears were even civilised – if the term is not just flattery.

It fuels my enthusiasm for trying to influence what happens in the wood. Paying grudging lip-service to the claims that observations on hand-reared animals give little indication of the behaviour of their truly wild relations, I decided to continue my experiments, on wild badgers, when the original cubs I had hand-reared were gone

Generations of field sportsmen, brought up to love the pleasures of the chase, are not the mindless vandals the trendies make them out to be. Catching a fox with a pack of hounds is not all about donning medieval hunting clothes and letting loose a hungry horde of ill-disciplined pooches. The huntsman needs to have them under control, to know where the quarry lives and be able to prevent his escape to some impregnable haven.

One way to accomplish at least the latter is to construct an artificial earth – or 'drain' – which is impregnable for most of the time, but the same retreat must be safe only when the fox is not being hunted. Then it must be impregnable – especially to foxes!

The way hunting men have accomplished this is to construct a subterranean den at the top of a bank which is entered by two tunnels constructed of drainpipes nine or ten inches in diameter which slope down, horseshoe fashion, from the den. The whole is covered with soil and turfed, in the green countryside, and partly so that the grass roots grow into a waterproof mat.

Foxes take to the artificial earths, or drains, as readily as tits to a nest box, and find them safe, warm and comfortable for most of the time. But, on the night before a meet of hounds, the terrier-man sends his terrier up one pipe to bolt the fox from his den and out the other. The terrier-man then blocks both entrances to the pipes so that, when hounds hunt the fox the following day and he flees for the safety of his drain, he finds himself blocked out and is forced to provide sport for the huntsmen by running the gauntlet to find another sanctuary.

Badgers find the same artificial earths as attractive as foxes do, so I built one in the bank above Primrose Dell, and I described the detailed construction in *Badgers at My Window*. The difference between my sett and drains constructed by the local hunt was that my badgers are never put under stress by being either blocked in or stopped out.

15. ON HOOF AND HOOK

My love of wildlife did not spring from the sensitivity of artists — for I am not artistic. Nor was it aroused by the clinical thirst for knowledge of scientists, for I have no time for those interested only in knowing more and more about less and less — until they know everything about nothing.

I was motivated as a child by the now discredited collector's urge, and the beetles I found I kept in boxes, and birds' eggs and butterflies in cabinets, which would not only be frowned on now but would be positively illegal.

I had so much pleasure, as a child, wandering among the pitbanks and other dereliction of worked-out coalmines, that aesthetic attractions were low among my priorities — which probably accounts for the fact that I was not in the least put off by the neglected woodland and almost derelict lodge I had bought. Real beauty lies beneath the skin. What mattered to me was that it was now possible to wander straight out of my own back door into quiet woodland where I was able to observe birds and beasts in my own time.

OPPOSITE The fallow bucks keep close to cover when strangers are about

The wild roe buck loved the woodland edge that bordered the paddock

Deer were high among these priorities. Gerald Springthorpe, who has been a close friend of more than thirty years, is now Wildlife Officer over a large tract of Forestry Commission lands from the Lake District to Bristol, but was then Deer Warden at Cannock Chase. He eats, dreams, thinks and sleeps deer and is an international authority on fallow deer so that I had long since been infected by his bug.

Some years previously I had hand-reared Dandy, a fallow buck fawn which made its debut on television, giving every sign of budding stardom. I then gave it to Frances Pitt whom I rate as the best all-round naturalist I have ever met and who was untold kind to Jess and me when we were young. I am proud that she did her first broadcast with me in the early 1950s and also her last shortly before she died a decade later. In fact, I was stupid to give her my fallow fawn because male deer grow up to be extremely dangerous and treacherous and Dandy set about Miss Pitt's companion when he sprouted antlers as a pricket. So we shipped him to Ireland to found a herd near Belfast and I hope he spiked some IRA before they got him.

The close association with Dandy and, later, with a delightful female roe deer I also reared on the bottle, cemented my affections — and greatly extended my knowledge. Before that, I had hugely enjoyed accompanying Gerald on dawn sorties on Cannock Chase in the hopes of catching a glimpse of fleeting forms which always seemed to be on the point of melting into the shadows.

Now I was able to sit up in bed and watch truly wild deer, feeding on the edge of our own wood, closer, more predictably and for longer periods than I had ever watched deer before. Friends, caught up in the frustrations of the urban rat-race, often agree that it is precisely the form of escape that they have dreamed about.

Butterflies are flamboyant and songbirds can fill our ears with pleasure, but deer are large enough and beautiful enough to fire childhood fantasies of *real*

His mate, my tame roe doe,
delighted us for ten years

wild animals. They are so emotive that well-balanced people, who believe that it is no business of theirs if friends enjoy hunting foxes or shooting pheasants, will lather themselves into a frenzy at the thought of noble deer being hunted with hounds. I share their sentiment because once, when the local MFH lost his hounds, they came into our wood, rioted onto our deer, and when I saw them pull one down I was powerless to stop them savaging her to death.

Yet I love an hour's ratting with my own dogs and don't have a qualm when they catch and kill their quarry. Perhaps it proves how illogical I am!

The snag, when we came here, was that there was absolutely nothing to stop *our* deer wandering off across the drive into my neighbour's equally unfenced wood where they immediately became *his* deer because wild animals belong to whoever owns the land they are on at the moment.

Since my neighbour's wood was leased interminably to the Forestry Commission and the Commission has the right to 'control' deer, there was nothing to stop them shooting my deer, a hundred yards from home across the drive! And if they got onto the farmland, the owner could shoot them, even out of season, if they were damaging his crops. So my initial relationship with the deer in the wood was deep affection, sharpened by anxiety for their safety. I felt fanatically protective!

Meanwhile, Brian Dale, my neighbour, viewed his newly-acquired estate of almost 2000 acres through very different eyes. Like me, he had bought the woodland in the full knowledge that the Forestry Commission had a lease for 999 years, at half a crown an acre – a thousand acres that would still only give a pittance of £125 a year to his great-grandson's grandson's heirs. Such rent would not be worth a postage stamp and would be a pathetic yardstick of how past landowners had dissipated their heritage.

Having made the pile he had invested in the land, Mr Dale wanted to make it work to gain more profit for further investments. Millionaires would not be millionaires without such motivation! Since half the estate was emasculated by the wretched Forestry lease, the other had has to work twice as hard, so his first act was to reclaim the deer park for agriculture. So it was only natural that he did not write welcome on his mat for deer to creep out of his own wood or mine to eat the corn which sprouted on his reclaimed land.

Nobody could say whether these plundering deer spent their daylight hours in his wood or mine but, since the Forestry Commission rented his wood, they were responsible for damage by deer living there, and the least pleasant part of Gerald's job was to cull them down to numbers small enough to cause no significant damage.

The hardwoods had been felled in the Forestry wood some years earlier, so a fair proportion of the local deer were lying up in my hardwoods and the birch thickets which were still waiting for Fred to clear as lop-and-top.

One day, therefore, I moved the deer across from our wood to Brian Dale's land where Gerald and a friend lay in wait with rifles. By the time I reached them, ten deer lay on the grass, dead but still warm, with undimmed, staring eyes.

The heat had been taken out of complaints of damaged crops – but the price, to me, was unacceptable. To grow crops next to ancient woodland inhabited by deer for centuries is like putting out a well-stocked bird-table in winter – and shooting the birds when they accept the invitation.

It was the first sour note to rattle through our wilderness and I determined to prevent a recurrence – but a way still had to be found to turn such theory into practice.

That first drastic cull shook me to the core and it took some time for the fact to dawn that population, of both man and beast, has to be kept in balance with the capacity of the habitat to support it. Advances in medical science have made human over-population one of the greatest problems of our time. With animals, it is easier to crop the surplus. So, each year we cull about 15% of our deer herd so that there is plenty for the rest to eat, and they stay 'on the hoof' to be admired. As a practical stockman, with the surplus end on the butcher's hooks, I have no qualms at all about relishing the venison they provide, conscious that they have lived a happy and dignified life. I would rather see a small herd of well-fed, happy deer than an army of hungry, half-fed brutes.

16. THE GILT WEARS OFF

There was, at that time, no prospect of being about to erect a deer-proof fence around our wood, for two reasons. I had only recently quit a well-paid job in industry, not so that I could cosily retire but in order to earn my living with my pen. And, as every freelance writer knows, that is a most precarious business because there is no way of controlling one's workload. Either too much lies ahead, with the danger of breaking sacrosanct deadlines – or too little, with even more imminent perils. So there was no income available to pay for an expensive fence and the capital we'd saved was needed elsewhere. At that stage, there was no prospect of the wood being self-supporting either although, in retrospect, I believe that that first unpleasant slaughter sowed the seed in my mind.

The other factor was the uncontrollable presence of Forestry Commission workers in our wood. They had, of course, an inalienable right to be there because they – or their successors – would be tenants until the year 2948. Fred Goodall was clearing his lop and-top in patches a few acres in extent. The Forestry workers followed him, starting in Lords Coppice, and methodically planted their miserable little softwoods. When the planting was completed, they would have to return occasionally to tend the young trees.

With very few exceptions, I have got on with them well but I am, by instinct, as territorial as a badger. Having just released myself from a long sentence in a factory, earning profits for my employers and being subjected to the ruthless competition to scramble at all costs to the top, I did not take kindly to strangers I was powerless to evict from my own patch!

But perhaps not quite powerless. Like most of his colleagues, the Forestry

e quiet and typically English
od in Holly Covert is a
ctuary for wildlife

ontrast, the sterile pines cast
much shade that few
tures choose to endure
r gloom

foreman was a decent chap, brought up in a placid, slow-motion rural trade where pressure and discord were the language of another world. Having industrial inoculations still coursing through my veins, I had no such inhibitions.

I explained to him that I had sweated my guts out for many years to save enough to stake my claim to a patch where I could repay my debts by making life more tolerable for the wildlife that I loved. Then I hammered the point home by making it clear that I had no intention of encouraging tenants to disturb the very creatures I had sacrificed to save.

I should therefore be grateful, I said, if he would not disturb the wood during the bird-nesting period in spring, or the 'fence month' — as June was called in medieval times — when shy deer were dropping their fawns. While he was at it, I continued, there would be great advantage if he kept his men out in October so the rutting deer would not be driven onto my millionaire neighbour's farmland. For good measure, I added, I would prefer my pheasants not to be driven over my boundary during the shooting season, that is October to February — and please don't walk through Holly Covert while the herons are nesting, that's from February to August.

Such demands were unreasonable and unacceptable because, if the poor chap had paid any attention, September was about the only month his men could have worked in the wood without complaint! But he was as anxious to cause no offence as only the nicest people are — and I was as hard-nosed as is the custom among successful businessmen. As a result, he compressed his men's visits into less than the minimum required for weed-free trees so that, on later occasions, there was less resistance to my requests for the Commission to disgorge their lease and return the control of the destiny of my land to me.

But that was years ahead. In the meantime, tens of thousands of trees were planted, mostly Corsican pine but some Scots pine and some Lodgepole. The foreman, despite my unwelcoming attitude, turned the other cheek by sparing quite a proportion of the larger birch and several stands of self-set oak in Lords Coppice which would otherwise have looked like an untidy desert with a stubble of pine trees which threatened to stifle all other growth beneath their canopy as they developed.

The immediate result of this forty acres of clear felling was to attract species which were not there before and with which I had never had personal contact. The most exciting were nightjars which nested in small numbers a mile away in similar terrain where the oaks of Bagot's Wood had been recently felled. Jess and I wandered out on summer evenings to listen to their drawn-out, vibrant churring which is not unlike the sound of a thumbnail being drawn across an exceptionally musical comb of almost infinite length. This churring song continues, neither rising nor falling in note or volume, for several minutes on end and, on one memorable night, we stood quite close to the songster, perched along the horizontal branch of an oak tree instead of conventionally across it. He burbled on for several consecutive minutes, appearing never to draw breath or open his beak, producing the sound with the effortless magic of a superb ventriloquist.

He eventually stopped and flew off into the dusk, 'hawking' flying moths and

A nightjar — a bird which prefers to live in scrubby woodland

other insects, wheeling and dodging unpredictably in relentless pursuit of his prey. When he had gone, the wood was still not silent because the air was filled with a tiny, almost inaudible echo of his song. It seemed as high-pitched as the squeal of bats and, less than twenty years later, my ears have dulled until they cannot distinguish either sound.

But in those days, the churring of nightjars in Lords Coppice and the minuscule song of grasshopper warblers made each evening sojourn in the wood an unforgettable experience. Both sounds drove home the lesson that nothing in the countryside is as it was for long. Before the oaks were felled, the habitat was suitable for neither grasshopper warblers nor nightjars. Both need very open woodland, the sites of newly-felled woods or scrubby common land. What made their short stay with us possible was the very clearing of mature trees and the associated lop-and-top to which I objected so strongly.

And as the young conifers grew and their branches joined in canopy, conditions changed once more to provide habitat that was inhospitable to such welcome visitors. It was an early lesson that proved that preservationists must fight a losing battle because they can't freeze the countryside into immobility at any stage of its development.

Some features wax at the expense of others. Some wane, however hard we try to fix them like a favourite photograph in an album. It made me realise that, if I hoped to encourage as many creatures as possible to inhabit the wood, the hard work was up to me. I had to try to manage the habitat to produce the whole gamut of stages from climax (mature and ancient) wood, as there is in Holly Covert, right through the cycle to newly-cleared sites like the Forestry Commission had provided in the course of their work in Lords Coppice.

The snag was, who would pay for it — and how could I gain possession of my leased land so that I could put into practice my ambitious dreams?

17. UNWELCOME GUESTS

Although the village ancients enthused about the culinary qualities of rabbits poached from our wood, there were precious few left when we arrived so that the nostalgic ramblings about what once had been rang pretty hollow.

Myxomatosis had taken a terrific toll in the 1950s and the few survivors grew even fewer because the locals gave them no peace to breed but harassed them seven days a week. Rabbiting is a traditional sport in the country and even when beaks on the bench are local landowners, they rarely slap on more than a piffling fine for even the most blatant poaching.

Local farmers' sons and their friends jumped on the wagon and bought powerful searchlights so that they could go 'lamping' at all hours of the night. Now they top up their nights out at the local pub with a spot of rabbit lamping, mechanising the sport by stripping the bodies from clapped-out jalopies on which they race across the fields, brandishing their weapons with the abandon of kids playing cowboys and indians. Their dazzled quarry is shot as it crouches or runs in the searchlight beam.

This goes on until one or two a.m., and then their mates from local towns are at it again by six or half past, including Sunday mornings. As one generation grows up and starts chasing wenches instead of more furry quarry, they are

Although England would not be home without a rabbit, neighbouring farmers beg to differ

replaced by younger friends and brothers who shatter what peace is left in the countryside.

But rabbits are survivors *par excellence* and, despite the dreaded past and visits from uninvited guests, the rabbit population has gradually recovered.

Academic scientists, who add strings of letters to their names by publishing learned papers, wrote thousands of words about the effect of myxomatosis on rabbits. Seven rabbits, they claimed, eat as much as a sheep so that turfland, grazed by huge numbers of rabbits, was cropped as short as the nap on a billiard table. The first waves of myxomatosis, in 1954, were said to have annihilated 99% of the rabbits where the population was densest.

No great powers of deduction were required to calculate that this would have a significant effect on rabbit numbers and scientific paper after scientific paper rolled off university printing presses, announcing that the demise of rabbits was resulting in great cosmetic changes to the landscape.

Hawthorn and blackberry seeds have always been excreted in the droppings of such birds as wood pigeons and blackbirds. These would have sprouted and sent down rootlets, as Nature intended, but then along came the rabbits, bit off the seedlings and ate them. Only very few survived to grow to maturity

Now that there weren't enough rabbits to eat them, heathland and downland turf, untouched by agriculture, sprouted into dense thickets of scrub which provided safety for creatures which could not have survived in the open – including rabbits. This had a knock-on effect because the rabbit pest is transmitted by inoculation by rabbit fleas. The fleas suck the blood of a stricken rabbit and infect the next victim they bite with their bloody mouths.

This is most likely to happen in densely populated rabbit warrens, where fleas survive in the luxury of warm dry bedding. But, given adequate cover and protection from predators, rabbits love lying out in 'sits', compressed in clumps of rushes or under bushes, and when they are so dispersed, it is obvious they are less likely to be bitten by a flea which has been feeding on an infected rabbit. Countrymen, noting their change of habitat and habits, call these creatures 'bush rabbits', and claim that they belong to a separate species.

These conditions were already present in Lords Coppice where Fred had cleared the lop-and-top and the Forestry Commission had planted seedlings by the time we arrived. Woodland soil, where undergrowth has been stifled for many generations by the shade and canopy of mature trees, still carries seeds which can remain viable for years and years.

The first season after a clearing is felled in our wood, there are dense stands of foxgloves, the seeds of which have been lying dormant there. Birch seedlings grow and the stools of felled birch coppice begin to sprout. Hazel bushes appear where no hazel was before and, in Lords Coppice, stands of seedling mountain ash appear. If there had been a large rabbit population, most of these would literally have been nipped off in the bud but, the felling coming so soon after myxomatosis had struck, the seedlings survived and, in time, provided refuge for the rabbits to recover as described above.

The poor chaps who had planted the Forestry seedlings were not so happy.

Men arrived in spring to chop
down everything but pine trees

A weed is often defined as a wildflower in the wrong place and, to them, the birch, bramble and mountain ash and any other plant that competed with their cherished pine trees were weeds! So gangs of men arrived, in spring, to chop down everything but pine trees. Not only did this so-called weeding disturb the nesting birds, it destroyed the very cover they needed to conceal their eggs and chicks, and obliterated the insect-food on which they fed.

It was a classic case of conflicting interests but since they had legally leased the land for a millennium they were in the right.

But right is not always might and, as I have said, the foreman was a thoroughly nice man who hated hurting anyone's feelings. We compromised, and he weeded his trees carefully where the cover my birds needed was not dense – which made the weeding easier – but he left quite large patches of bramble, bracken and thicket in between, like the squares on a draught board. Accordingly, the patches of undergrowth helped the rabbits recover from the plague more easily.

One of these rabbits had established his territory at the far end of Lords Coppice, about half a mile from the house. He was as black as a golliwog, and interested me a great deal. I thought little about this oddity at first, for I concluded it was simply an escapee from some child's rabbit hutch, although the nearest children lived more than a mile away in the village. So, if it had been a pet, either someone local had set it free or it had had a good walk across hostile terrain.

The rabbit survived for more than a year, which the boffins say is a long span for wild rabbits, and then it disappeared. But it was not very long before another black rabbit replaced it and one or two after that. Then myxomatosis struck again, wiping most of them out, though not as high a percentage as the first time. We've had the plague four or five times, over the years, and although each new wave has been less lethal than the last, the percentage of casualties has still been very high.

After each bout, we have always noticed the odd black survivor, though whether this is because each wave of the disease is weaker than the last or because surviving rabbits develop immunity has never been made clear. Since odd colours are normally due to recessive genes, I was surprised they had not 'bred themselves out'.

In theory, rabbits are unwelcome guests because neighbouring farmers, past masters in the art of finding things to grumble about, whinge a bit about the rabbits which, if one believes the farmers' theories, must eat a ton of corn a day! My own view is that anyone who buys or rents a farm on inhospitable ground like ours, bordered by a wood, should expect a few unwanted guests to share his crop. It was probably one of the reasons the estate's price was low in the first place.

For my part, I know they do a bit of damage by nipping regenerating saplings in the bud – but they also provide an alternative diet which takes some of the pressure off pheasants and wildlife like voles and woodmice that would otherwise be decimated by foxes and other predators. Anyway, the place wouldn't be the same for me without a few rabbits coming out to feed at dusk. They were among the attractions that first caught our eye and I should hate to lose them all.

18. IN DEFENCE OF HERONS

Although the Bagot goats had annihilated the holly trees which gave Holly Covert its name, the initial attraction there was the colony of herons.

In contrast, by far the greatest worry was the flocks of crows which assembled there to roost. The time to get them in perspective was the first half-hour of darkness on frosty winter evenings. The crows were, in fact, the last arrivals. Jackdaws came in first. About four o'clock on January afternoons, the first scouts drifted across the evening sky, silhouetted by the ball of yellow setting sun which makes sunset, through the brittle branches of the stag-headed oaks on my neighbour's forty acres, so truly memorable.

These feathered outriders were smaller than carrion crows, with puny voices as squeaky as a eunuch's. They alighted, complaining falsetto about everything and everyone, sitting high up on their vantage boughs until they had satisfied themselves that no danger lurked. Then they drifted across the drive to check in for the night in the tallest birches in Holly Covert.

Birdwatching friends, used to the fact that suitable habitat for jackdaws is steadily shrinking, assured me how lucky I was that they were prepared to be guests while I assumed the role of host. Having grown up with keepers who shot, trapped and poisoned all corvids 'on suspicion', I was not so sure.

Jackdaws love eggs, and the undergrowth in our wood was sparse enough to make any nest of blackbird or mistlethrush, willow warbler or turtle dove,

Jackdaws, in high-pitched chorus, come in first to roost – and stay in spring to breed

moorhen, pheasant or wild duck stick out like a sore thumb. It was obvious that we were in for more than enough trouble from the resident plague of magpies and jays, without encouraging these grey-headed black varmints!

The cause of their high numbers was obvious. Until our neighbour reclaimed his deer park for agriculture, it had been liberally spattered with venerable but decrepit ancient oaks. These stubby survivors of previous fellings had been left because they were split or hollow or too knotty to be worth sending to the sawmill. But they were exactly the habitat hole-nesting birds such as owls and jackdaws would specify as 'five-star'. As a result, the trees had, for generations, been positively sniving with jackdaws which had flown out in clouds if anyone had hit the trunk with a heavy stick or lobbed a stone into the labyrinth of crevices.

When these trees had been uprooted and heaped on their funeral pyres, literally hundreds of jackdaws had been dispersed about the surrounding countryside in search of other lodgings. How far they had to go to satisfy their reproductive drive, I have no means of knowing but, outside the breeding season ever since, they and their descendants have congregated to roost in Holly Covert. This was the nearest standing woodland to their ancient territory from which they were driven by 'advances' in modern agriculture.

The arrival of flocks of roosting jackdaws seems to act as a catalyst to stimulate their distant relatives into a similar nightly pattern. Flocks of rooks follow suit first and, while the light is fading from dusk to dark, an almost continuous queue of much larger black birds drifts in to roost on topmost branches, picked out stark and forbidding against the evening sky. The fact that they are bigger helps to distinguish them from the smaller jackdaws because by the time they arrive, the light has faded too much for it to be possible to see if they have the grey heads or eyes of jackdaws.

It would, of course, be easy enough to confuse them with carrion crows but their characteristic cawing puts a seal on their identity. I am particularly fond of rooks, and loved the small rookery in the limes at the Cottage where we lived before here; I am ever hopeful that some of the birds which accept the hospitality here of a comfortable roost, free from interference, will decide one year to stay on and start a rookery over the peninsula on Dunstal Pool, which is just the sort of place that rooks might choose.

Every spring, I intend to go out on about the 10th of May to any rookery in the district and pick up half a dozen fledglings which always seem to fall out of the nest around that date, which is before they are able to fly. But I never get around to it. Having hand-reared a couple of albinos – and an ordinary black chap when I was at school – I know from experience how easy it would be to rear them. Kept in an aviary until they are old enough to support themselves, there is a reasonable chance that they might settle here and breed – but Murphy's Law being what it is, the odds on them being shot by neighbours before they reach maturity have so far put me off. So the project must wait for the combination of a spell working at home – to cover the vital hand-rearing period – and the time when the local lads grow up to become hunters of more sophisticated quarry. Now the trespassers are curbed, a new generation is unlikely to replace them.

Neither the jackdaws nor the rooks are really unwelcome in the wood, if only because they mostly disperse during the day to the surrounding countryside to pick up a living.

The birds I do dislike – and I dislike *very* few wild creatures – are the carrion crows that come in last. Every man's hand is against carrion crows, with good reason. They will peck the eyes out of lambs, or lacerate their tongues, while the ewe is helpless in the act of giving birth; I have watched a pair of crows hunt and kill leverets only a few hours old; and they take the eggs and chicks from anything from song or game birds to domestic poultry.

My immediate worry about them in Holly Covert is the eggs and chicks in the heronry there. Oddly enough, herons seem able to look after themselves if they are left entirely alone. I have watched, at a distance through powerful field glasses, a belligerent old heron standing on her nest, defying the crows to come within striking distance of her beak. The wily birds knew better!

The danger arises when someone, however innocently, disturbs the herons and drives them off their nests, which is perilously easy to do. It only needs an uninvited guest, simply enjoying the country, going for a walk or hoping to take photographs, to come into view. The great birds, deeming discretion the better part of valour, immediately fly out of gunshot range. The opportunist crows nip in and make a snatch before the rightful occupants return.

So I take action before the herons return to breed. When the jackdaws and rooks have settled for the night, the crows come in, in dozens and scores, to join them. After a war of attrition that has lasted since we came, the crows still

When there are no trigger-happy humans to cause disturbance, herons are capable of seeing off crows and other feathered robbers

persist so I sometimes go up the wood with my rifle, hoping to silhouette a black varmint in my telescopic sight against the moon. The silencer – or 'sound moderator' as the bumblese on the licence describes it – reduces the report to a dull plop, hopefully followed by a slightly duller plop as the victim hits the ground.

It is like extracting the legendary dragon's teeth, for as fast as one is killed, he is replaced by twelve more. But repeated forays with my rifle before the herons return each spring eventually have the effect of making most of the crows so spooky that at least some of them go elsewhere, to bother someone else. The worst aspect is that it is almost impossible to control those crows which stay to breed in the wood and are present to wreak havoc in the hours of daylight. As fast as I shoot one, he is replaced by another from the reservoir of roosting birds, so that, try as I might, the wood always seems to hold the optimum – which is crow language for maximum – number of breeding pairs.

19. NO END TO THE TUNNEL

The pleasures of escape from working in a factory to the solitude of our wilderness would have been sharper if it had been possible to be more aware of what actually went on in the wood. But it soon became clear that, far from living *in* the wood and sharing it with the native wildlife there, we were still outsiders, living on the edge that divided intensively-worked farmland from what we hoped would prove to be primeval forest.

Although we owned the wood, there were the unacceptable strangers to the resident birds and beasts – namely the woodmen who tended the seedling trees, and the locals who resented the fact that they were no longer unchallenged if they strayed over the boundary with loaded guns in search of illicit sport.

The Lodge was situated in the south-west corner of a paddock which was bounded on the south by Dunstal Pool and to the north and east by thick willow and larch scrub at the edge of Dunstal Pool Plantation and the southern tip of Holly Covert, which are both about a hundred yards from the sitting-room window. If we had bought any cottage, with a paddock of an acre or two bounded by an impenetrable hedge, the view could have been just as restricted.

The one chink of light was the main extraction ride, along which a small caterpillar crawler dragged load after load of felled tree trunks from Lords Coppice and Longlands to the drive above the house. This woodland ride happened to cleave a straight path from the north corner of Lords Coppice, between the boundaries of Longlands and Cockshutt Close, pointing straight at the sitting-room window. At sunset, the golden rays lit it as we sat watching the duck on Dunstal Pool. At dawn, we could lie in bed above and watch as the horizontal winter sunbeams in the ride winkled the sleep from our eyes.

This was obviously a key woodland ride for it was the only one so far that penetrated more than a hundred yards in a straight line into the wood. We could see movement at the far end about six hundred yards away, so my first task was to persuade the Commission foreman not to plant any of his little trees actually on the ride and, if possible, to leave a yard or so each side unplanted so that, in years to come, the growing pine branches would not join in a canopy to blot out the ride.

But looking up this ride, from my study or the sitting-room, was like peering into the wood through a narrow gap in a hedge, because the birch and willow at the edge of Dunstal Pool Plantation and on the peninsula above the pool itself gave just that impression, so to open up the view I started to cut it away with a four-foot bow saw.

Two days – and two blistered palms – later, it was almost impossible to see where I had been. A nibbling buck rabbit could scarcely have made less impression.

This should not have surprised me because I had been a founder member – and later president – of our County Conservation Trust, and one of the functions of such bodies is to marshal squads of eager beavers to do scrub clearance, pool cleaning and similar boring but vital chores on nature reserves owned, or leased, by the Trust. On Saturday afternoons and Sundays, these well-meaning enthusiasts turn out, often unsuitably dressed and wielding unfamiliar scythes and sickles, pickaxes and crowbars, spades and other hand-blistering implements, to do battle with the elements.

Too often the results are as pathetic as mine were on the edge of Dunstal Pool but sore hands, aching muscles and sweaty shirts hold no thrills for me, so I hung my bow saw on its hook and borrowed my neighbour's tractor and a stout steel chain with a hook on each end.

Fixing a loop round any sapling up to three or four inches in diameter, four or five feet from the ground, and the other hook onto the drawbar of the tractor, I drove steadily away on the tractor, being careful not to snatch the chain. The chain tightened and the sapling bent to take the strain. The tractor did not check but continued on its remorseless way. The sapling contorted and creaked – and gave up its hold on life. The tractor heaved it – and another and another – out by its roots as easily as I can hand-weed a bed of nettles. I dragged them into a pile where fire consumed them as cleanly as Fred burned lop-and-top so that, in the time it would have taken me to clear a few square yards, the fringe of willow scrub had made way for satisfying vistas into the wood.

Most conservation trusts number among their members a farmer or two because, contrary to popular belief, a high percentage of farmers are keen naturalists who wish to leave the land better than they found it. So, instead of denigrating the good with the small number of vandal exceptions, it might be profitable for naturalist trusts to cultivate the farmers on the Old Boy basis, for the loan of

Looking back to the Lodge
through an early woodland ride

a tractor and driver would do more good work in an afternoon than a van-load of enthusiastic amateurs.

That first long ride cleared up to the softwood in Lords Coppice, plus the reasonably open chinks into the hardwood near the pool, only emphasised how little we could actually see from the house. The newly planted pines were so small that they barely poked their leaders above the grass, but it was all too clear that, within a very few years, they would grow into an impenetrable grey-green mass which would obliterate everything more than three or four hundred yards from the window, where Longlands and Cockshutt Close joined the pool plantation. There was nothing I could do about it unless I could regain possession of the land leased by the Forestry Commission and, as it was firm Commission policy to hang on to what they held, it seemed an impossible dream.

The only glint of hope lay in a senior official whom I had known well since we had been founder members of the Mammal Society; he was, I knew, a first-rate, dedicated naturalist. When I broached the subject with him, he expressed his sympathy but explained the impossibility because it would create a precedent which would incite every other landowner with land let at a similar confiscatory rent of half a crown an acre to expect similar treatment.

Making the ride to Primrose Dell, half a mile away

20. SMALL MERCIES

The notion of regaining possession of our land had seemed to be such an impossible fantasy that I buried it at the back of my mind, with other passing whims. We had not arrived with any grandiose schemes for putting the world to rights, but had simply done what so many others would like to do and escaped from modern pressures to what we believed would simply be the simple life.

As a freelance writer and broadcaster, I could not control the volume of my work input, so I had to grab what opportunities were offered — I then used whatever surplus creative energy was left to make other opportunities to grab!

I have always been a firm believer in the Old Boy network and in having as wide a circle of friends and acquaintances as possible. Jess is a highly competent cook and first-rate hostess so that she more than pulls her weight in the team. But the basic stock-in-trade of any writer is his subject matter, and our wood was to be the basic material to supply our inky living. So many people write about what others have said or done that I reckoned I could cut the competition by describing personal experience instead.

Wandering round a wood overgrown with bracken, reeds and general undergrowth kicks up so much disturbance that wildlife has every chance to be forewarned and make itself scarce long before there is any chance to see it. For this reason, anything of interest spotted on country walks is more by luck than plan, and past experience had taught me that the easiest way to discover what's around is to select a likely spot — and keep perfectly still. After a while, when there has been time to merge with the surroundings, animals and birds forget there is a stranger in their midst, and carry on living where they left off. Even so, it is necessary to choose a spot which is not too overgrown to offer any view — and if it is possible to get there unobtrusively, so much the better.

So I decided to start by cutting a few small woodland rides round Holly Covert where I was in total control and had neither Commission tenants nor anyone else to say me nay. Scientists talk knowingly about the 'woodland edge effect', explaining that a very high percentage of wildlife, from birds to butterflies, inhabits the edge of woodland more densely than thickets in the centre. This is not the blinding discovery that pompous pundits pretend. A moment's reflection will show that air currents and direct sunlight, uninhibited by undergrowth, are likely to be more beneficial to a wider range of vegetation than the shady canopy of interlacing branches. And the greater the variety of vegetation in places like open rides, the more likely it is that a wide range of wildlife will choose to live, feed and breed there.

We had bought an Allen scythe to mow awkward patches round the pool at the Cottage, so I cleaned and oiled and fettled it up. It is a motorised scythe, with oscillating 'fingers', like the lethal contraptions fitted to mowing machines used to cut the hay. But, instead of attaching it to a tractor, which is powerful enough to discipline its cavorting eccentricities, I was condemned to walk behind my motorised machine, steering it as best I could by two large handles. To describe

We often get exotic surprises, such as this Pale Tussock caterpillar

By cutting small rides in the wood, we can get around quietly without creating disturbance

it as putting the cart before the horse was an understatement because, in this case, the powerful motor drove the cart — or mower — and I was the horse, not propelling it but doing my feeble best to dictate roughly where it went.

Seeing workers in public parks or along road verges walking sedately behind such implements, leaving level swath after parallel swath to mark their passing, conveys quite the wrong impression.

I had no level sward to mow, but was condemned to attack the virgin, tussocky, tree-rooted mass of an untamed wood. The machine was so powerful that the knives sliced through saplings as thick as walking sticks if they happened to be where the centre of the machine was going. If, however, a sapling or unusually tough clump of reed or bush happened to coincide with the end of the cutting knife, the whole machine lurched off on a quite different course which was far beyond my puny strength to control. It was rather like being matched with a robot all-in wrestler who heaved his victims over the equivalent of untamed ploughland, instead of amusing the crowd by chucking them through the ropes.

The one compensation was that the agony was over more quickly than if conventional brushing and slashing hooks had been used. Half a day cutting paths with the old motor scythe took six hot baths and a week off at my desk before stiffness eased and, on one occasion, the cure was far more drastic than that.

I had been cutting a path through bracken where Holly Covert joins Daffodil Lawn and, since the bracken would be four feet high by July, I decided to retrace my steps until I'd cut three swaths wide, to avoid the cover on each side subsiding to conceal the path I'd cut. On the second time up, I felt a sharp pain on the back of my hand, cursed the bramble thorns I hadn't noticed, and carried on, hot, sweaty and bad tempered.

Only on my return journey did I discover that I hadn't been jagged by a rebel bramble but warned off the territory of a swarm of wasps. The chattering steel blades of the mower had sliced through their nest and the surviving wasps were lying in ambush for my return, and were very cross indeed.

I bumbled innocently into the waiting swarm which set about me in the meanest fashion. They got in my hair and up my sleeves and in my shirt, and I left the whirring machine to look after itself and went for home full tilt. Luckily I had a pair of wellies on, and keep my trousers up with a leather belt, so I didn't get stung too vitally. But I clocked up over forty stings on the rest of my person which poisoned me so badly that whole areas went wooden and I had to go to the doctor. It taught me a lot about wasps — and did nothing to increase my affection for hand-controlled motor scythes.

I am more mechanised now, but when I was still using the old Allen, I cut a total of more than six miles of pathway through the wood and the network of little rides I cut in Holly Covert were the prototypes of rides I have since extended through the wood so that I can mooch off quietly with the dogs at heel, and get to the most obscure places without causing any disturbance. I imagine I also encourage more plants to spread because of the 'woodland edge effect' the scientists rave about! It was certainly doing things the hard way — but it would have been even harder without such minimal mechanisation!

21. KITTED UP

When Fred Goodall finished clearing up the lop-and-top in Lords Coppice, it was the end of an era for him. He had worked on farms before the war but, when he was invalided out of the army, after being wounded at Tobruk, he decided to be his own master and work for himself. He bought a tractor and trailer and contracted to clear the lop-and-top, after the timber-fellers had finished taking trees, and made his money by selling logs.

Lords Coppice was the last standing timber in the area for which there was any chance of getting a felling licence so, when it was all cleared, Fred took up hedging and tree-felling and other skilled jobs for which there is always a demand in the country. His new clients had tractors of their own so he sold his to me.

It had first been licensed in 1957 so it was then seven years old and past its pristine youth – but it was the beginning of an era for me. I paid Fred £100 for it and it has had one overhaul in the meantime which cost another hundred, so it doesn't owe me much and is still as good as ever. Those old grey Fergies are superb tools and have one incomparable advantage.

As farm mechanisation increases and fields get bigger, little Ferguson tractors, like mine, would seem like tom tits on a round of beef if set to plough a prairie field. So would the implements which went with them, with the result that they sell for a song at any farm sale. One rude fellow told me that the number plate of 559 RRE would fetch more than the tractor was worth if I sold it to a status-conscious chap who wanted a prestigious personalised number plate. I got my own back by buying from him for a tenner a single furrow plough to fit the tractor because he couldn't find anyone else who still used a tractor small enough to fit it. Not that I do much ploughing, but it comes in handy when I wish to erect a length of rabbit-proof fencing. I plough one furrow in which I bury the bottom of the netting, thereby effectively stopping the rabbits creeping under it.

Over the years, I've got very well kitted up with implements to fit the tractor. Tom Blore, our local blacksmith, is young in years but comes of generations of smiths. Working for his father, Fred, for a few seasons knocked him into the shape of a real craftsman which, sadly, is now a rarity in the countryside. Tom made me a roller which can be used empty or filled with water, so I can choose whether to go over the ground with five hundredweights or a ton, and he made a carrier to fit the hydraulics that is perfect for carrying huge loads of light material, such as leaves or hay, over ground so fugged that a trailer would get stuck. The light finger mower is just the job for topping the rough grass from wide rides and clearings – provided you look out for lurking tree roots – and I swapped an old circular saw for an enormous hay rake that will clear the cut grass in a couple of passes.

I have an ancient scuffle that is quite efficient at grubbing patches of bracken and feg, almost as the pigs would do, leaving turned-up soil to help regeneration, but the best tool of all is my swipe.

When windblown trees are no good for fencing posts, they keep us warm in winter on log fires

I traded a set of disc harrows for a carcase of venison

Foxes don't spend all their time in earths – they also enjoy sunbathing in secluded places

It is a macho vandal with stupendous powers of destruction. Basically, it consists of three very heavy chains, suspended from a vertical shaft which is driven by the hydraulic drive of the tractor. When in gear, with the engine turning over fast, the spindle rotates and swings the chains like an unstoppable, horizontal propeller. The chains can be adjusted to rotate anything from ground level to a few inches clear, and they lop off everything which gets in their way. At ground level, they will cut grass as short as a conventional mowing machine, though they tear it off rather than cutting cleanly. But grass is only a beginning. Driving the tractor through shoulder-high bracken, it leaves a swath of battered leaves as if it had been scythed. I can drive it into an apparently inpenetrable bramble brake and emerge the other side with, behind me, a barbered path four feet wide which is thereafter comfortable to walk on. Saplings anything up to an inch thick are just as vulnerable so that a path through a birch thicket takes only as long as it takes to drive the tractor through in bottom gear.

If it consisted of nothing but the three chains rotated by the drive shaft, it would be suicide to drive because, when a chain comes into contact with a stone, it swings it away, quite haphazardly, with the velocity of a Roman catapult. Anyone stopping the stone would be felled as surely as David felled Goliath, so the whole contraption is sheathed in a case of heavy-gauge steel sheet. Driving across rough ground, the pebbles hit this sheath with the melodic clangs of a peal of cathedral bells and the beauty is that, if the chain does hit an immovable root, it only loops and unfurls instead of breaking a blade as would happen with a conventional mower.

The swipe came from a government surplus sale and the whole set of tractor-driven equipment cost less than the price of a new Allen scythe, which has now been relegated to small spaces where it is not possible to work the tractor. Indeed, money did not even pass in every case because I managed to swap a first-class disc harrow for a carcase of venison when we were culling deer one year.

Next to the swipe, this disc harrow is perhaps the most useful tool because it is perfect for levelling rides cut to ribbons by the contractors lugging out timber, and the ruts can be smoothed with the water roller in the first fine spell after I've disced the ground.

The fact that I need to employ no permanent labour is due partly to the fact that the really big operations, such as thinning and felling timber, are done by contractors who pay me to take it out, while I can manage the maintenance work in what spare time I have. Writing and broadcasting are very unpredictable and, while I have been writing this book, I have worked a seven-day week for several months. I have got my regular assignments pretty well taped so that I normally reckon to be able to get every Saturday off. And from when the clock goes on, in April, until the nights draw in, I reckon to have an hour or so in the wood nearly every evening.

If I had to do my jobs by hand, as members of the natural history societies normally do, I should never have a spare hour to enjoy the fruits of my labours. Getting properly kitted out, with ancient but serviceable equipment, has made all the difference between a pleasure and a chore. All-in wrestling bouts with the bucking Allen scythe are now rare, while forays with a hand scythe are non-events.

I sit, instead, on the cushioned seat of my trusted Fergie and it is quite astonishing what I see while I am working. Wild animals seem not to associate mechanical noise and movement with any sort of danger. Tractor drivers who are ploughing fields frequently notice that a hare, jugging in a furrow, will not trouble to move out of the way until the wheels are nearly on top of her. The impersonal, snorting machine has been so long getting nearer by the furrow width that the hare has long since written it off as harmless.

I find the same thing with our deer. Going round the edge of the wood, mowing the rides, I often spot deer lying up chewing their cud. Their jaws stop masticating for a few seconds as I approach the first time, but begin to chew again almost before I am past. After another circuit or so, they don't even have the manners to pause while I pass. On one occasion, I even passed close by a fox, sunning himself on the bank of Primrose Dell. In the hour or so between tea and supper, I can deal with all the patches of bracken I want to crush in order to give more delicate plants a chance and, although the big jobs, like mowing the deer glade, can take half a Saturday, it only has to be done about three times each summer.

I regard my Fergie almost as a personal friend for, without him, life would not be half the fun, and occasional opportunities to procure some new implement, at bargain price, delight the latent wheeler-dealer in my soul.

22. OFFICIAL RECOGNITION

Holly Covert did not only harbour crows and jackdaws and other unwelcome guests, but it was also the breeding ground for a large number of herons who moved here when their traditional heronry had fallen to the woodman's axe. This had hit the headlines locally because, so rumour had it, a prominent local birdwatcher had married into the family of the Top Brass of the Nature Conservancy Council. The story went that this worthy had been very cross indeed when his son-in-law's bird-ringing activities had come to a sudden halt through destruction of the herons' nests.

It is rarely possible to test the substance of such stories because they are instinctively denied, but the fact remains that the news that I intended to provide sanctuary for the birds had the effect of sweet oil on troubled waters.

Goat Lodge was a listed building so that any planning application for alterations had to be referred to 'London', but I gathered that, if 'London' was obstructive, I would be able to build a Warden's Cottage instead — so long as the birds were safe. When they were well settled in, in the summer of 1968, a letter arrived from the Nature Conservancy Council to reward me. This announced that the

The heronry in Holly Covert

whole ninety acres of our wood, pools and pasture had been scheduled as a Site of Special Scientific Interest. The scientifically interesting features were enumerated as the heronry, the colony of wild daffodils on Daffodil Lawn, and some bogbean, growing in Dunstal Pool.

Bogbean is shown, in the *Flora of Staffordshire*, as being fairly widely distributed in 'acid pits, reed swamps and moorland bogs' and scarcely seemed to me to qualify as being specially scientifically interesting. It may be no coincidence that I had mentioned bogbean casually in a 'Living World' Nature Trail. The producer had thought it just the thing to liven up proceedings because I had fallen head first into the pool while picking a piece from the water. As Dunstal Pool is fed by water draining over the oak leaf-mould and bracken peat in Holly Covert, the water is almost acid enough to top up tractor batteries, so bogbean is not a particularly surprising plant to find there. In any case, it was all eaten by Canada geese next season so its fame was pretty transitory!

The colony of wild daffs on Daffodil Lawn was truly delightful – and they certainly did need protection; in the past, they had caused so much trespass that our predecessor had chain-harrowed them every spring to try to remove temptation.

But Sites of Special Scientific Interest are supposed to protect natural important habitat which has not changed significantly over the generations. Ancient woodland, like the Forest of Needwood, or 'semi-natural' woodland, which may have been influenced by cropping but still retains indigenous plants, are cases in point. Hardwoods which have been clear-felled and replaced by foreign pines are not. The most cursory inspection of Daffodil Lawn reveals evidence of the ancient traditional ridge-and-furrow ploughing, suggesting that, however 'wild' the wild daffs are, someone planted them deliberately in the first place. There are no others like them in the area, which lends substance to the theory.

The Nature Conservancy survey, before scheduling the SSSI, did not even mention the wild service trees which really are symptomatic of truly ancient woodland, and are also at the edge of the Lawn (*see* page 139).

The oaks in Holly Covert were vital for the heron nests, but were by no means 'natural' woodland. Once more, the contours of the land indicated the presence of ancient ridge-and-furrow ploughing – and the tree trunks were in lines along the tops of the ridges, so it was hardly likely that the acorns had been planted by squirrels! Judging by the fairly uniform size of the trees, I should guess they were planted about a century and a half ago, when the Lodge (then called Woodman's Cottage) was built, so their claim to special scientific interest was pretty tenuous too.

Inclusion of the forty acres leased for a thousand years to the Forestry Commission put on the final seal of lunacy. What hardwoods there had been had been clear-felled and replaced by sterile, foreign pines, and there was nothing the NCC could – or at any rate would – do to influence the way the Forestry cultivated it.

In spite of all this, they lumped the whole wood into a scheduled Site of Special Scientific Interest – and who was I to look such a gift horse in the mouth? So far as I was concerned, it would give at least some nominal protection by lending weight to objections to local changes of land-use that might affect the wildlife here. The NCC would have to be 'consulted' before such planning consent was granted – although they too had no really effective teeth if it came to the crunch.

The significant result of having the wood officially recognised was to put the whole project in perspective. Initially, the euphoria about protecting the persecuted herons, and the genuflections this generated from officialdom, almost had me convinced that, far from pursuit of simple pleasures, we were embarking on some sort of visionary crusade to which all must be sublimated.

The man from the Nature Conservancy Council was obviously a nice fellow who meant well, though he was a trifle patronising about the lofty importance of being specially scientifically interesting. To be scheduled by him appeared to be as good as a tap on the shoulder from the royal sword.

In the cold light of day, such intemperance was as obviously over the top as grounds for scheduling the place at all. The plain fact was that the land we had purchased was a very ordinary wood, with pleasant, relatively isolated farmland on three sides and a very large wood on the fourth, which in turn merged with an even larger tract that had once been the Forest of Needwood. The nice thing was that Jess and I had fallen in love with it as we found it – warts and all – and we needed no artificial accolade to be able to enjoy it.

The purpose of scheduling an area as a Site of Special Scientific Interest is to try to prevent important natural habitat being destroyed by modern threats. Chemical and mechanised farming have created such fundamental changes in the countryside that whole species of animals and birds, plants and insects are threatened with extinction. Worthy attempts to preserve them, by embalming whole slices of habitat in an artificial shroud of protection, have no more chance of success than Canute had of stemming the tide.

To be honest, one could not really understand why our wood had been scheduled as such a site because its claim to ancient continuity had been rubbished by our predecessors who had felled the area of indigenous Needwood Forest. From the purist viewpoint, they had compounded the felony by ploughing the cleared land, sowing grass on Daffodil Lawn and planting oak trees along the ridges in Holly Covert.

The wild service tree on Daffodil Lawn (on the beech's right) is a relic of the ancient woodland of olden times

The landowner who had blued a fortune to build a grandiose gothicised cottage to inflate the importance of his park may well have planted the original 'wild' daffodils as icing to his cake. Pressure from on high to preserve the newly-settled heronry had produced exceptional, if illogical, motivation from the nice man at the Nature Conservancy Council!

23. THE FENCE

Fond as I am of dogs, I confess to uncharitable thoughts towards several pooches from the village. The executive belt which now slumbers in the country and commutes to city offices has a nasty habit of buying a Lab or Hunt Terrier, to provide a with-it image at weekends, with the minimum trouble during the week. Such ignorant newcomers sometimes start by shutting the dog in the house during the time the family is at work or school. When they discover that bored dogs while away the lonely hours by chewing the carpet – or soaking it in urine or worse – they lock the dog *out*, to find its own amusement during working hours.

One such idle hound may be fairly harmless and confine himself to chasing neighbours' cats or burying bones in their gardens. Two are the nucleus of a feral pack and will soon start to wander in search of suitable quarry.

We erected heavy gauge fencing to keep deer in and hounds and trespassers out

Although we live a mile from the village, wayward stray dogs seemed to have an instinctive knack of wandering in our direction. The first we would know about it would be a flurry of deer in all directions, and a moment's pause would usually reveal two stray dogs in hot pursuit. One rarely seemed to hunt on its own. The dogs seldom caught a deer, but they drove them out of our wood, either into the Big Wood, Brian Dale's 1000 acres across the drive, or onto neighbouring farmers' crops.

Some owners were so stupid that they rather approved of this because it saved them having to give the dog a daily walk for exercise and, anyway, 'it was natural and the dog enjoyed it'. They thought that I was being very stuffy by objecting to their doggy chasing the deer, hares and rabbits in my wood and that farmers were narrow-minded and mean to grudge the deer a mouthful of tender crops.

The law, as happens all too often, is an ass where trespass is concerned. A deer or other game, *when unenclosed*, is a wild animal in the eyes of the law, and the law also reckons it 'natural' for dogs to hunt wild animals.

I am far too fond of dogs to shoot them for behaving naturally and would far prefer to put my boot in the seat of their owner's pants. Tough, the Alsatian we had when we came, was very hard-mouthed with canine rivals on her territory, and Belle, my present bitch, does not draw the line at killing them. So we had – and still do have occasionally – bloody battles in the wood, but it was an unwinnable war when the boundary fence was anything but dog-proof.

The most essential quality of any wildlife reserve is seclusion from disturbance. Gamekeepers would rather have the odd lone poacher, whom they will probably catch in due course, than gaggles of woolly-hatted ramblers traipsing and chattering through their coverts. If they take undisciplined dogs with them, their felony is compounded. Precisely the same is true of shy birds and beasts which thrive on a sense of security, as we do, but up sticks and vanish if disturbed, particularly by errant dogs.

So Jess and I discussed the possibility of putting a secure, dog-proof fence round the whole wood. The more we got down to brass tacks, the more impractical it seemed. The boundary was over 3000 yards or about a mile and three quarters long. That would take the cost of netting into four figures — not counting the support posts or the labour of erection.

We chewed it over, growing increasingly determined. At first we thought we should be able to do it by sacrificing our holiday. While I was working in industry, our annual holidays had consisted of a couple of weeks in some quiet fishing hotel — not because we liked fishing but because such places are usually in lovely country and attract pleasant fellow guests. But such holidays are relatively cheap and saving on one would not even dent the outlay required for the fence. So we decided to put as many holidays in hock as the netting cost would take, for, living and working in such surroundings, who needs a holiday?

Working on the principle that you get only what you pay for, we decided to purchase the very best quality we could afford rather than buy rubbish on the cheap which would rust away and require renewing before we'd turned our backs. We settled on very heavy gauge weldmesh, with six-inch-square mesh which was large enough for rabbits, foxes and pheasants to pass through, but too small for anything but tiny dogs.

While I had served my time in industry, I had been trained as a work study engineer and knew a bit about economy of effort and the advantages of mechanising to limit labour-intensive operations which are exceptionally costly.

The task of digging a heavy support post two feet into virgin ground, every five or six yards for a mile and a half, was pretty daunting. So I decided we would not dig them in. We would hire a mechanical JCB digger which could start by shoving its bucket along the boundary, providing a level surface to take the base of the netting. Every five yards, a labourer could hold a post vertical where it was due to be erected, and the man with the digger could put his loaded bucket on top of the post and squeeze it down into the soil by brute force.

It worked like a charm — and was most impressive to watch. Cleft oak posts, eight feet six inches high, simply sank into the ground until only six feet protruded by nothing but irresistible power. What is more, there was no loose soil to be rammed solid, as there is when conventional post holes are dug, so that every post stood rock steady and immovable.

When a line of posts fifty yards long had been erected, one end of a roll of netting was stapled to the end post and the netting unrolled. We made a clamp to hold the other end, attached it to a heavy chain and, with a powerful ratchet, pulled the whole thing as taut as violin strings. All that was then necessary was to fix it with staples to each intervening post — and a fifty-yard stretch was done.

It cost far less than we had feared, though we took the risk of using netting which was only four feet high and topping it with two strands of high-tensile barbed wire, making the fence effectively six feet tall. This was virtually unclimbable for human trespassers, and stray dogs very rarely got in — though we had to check that badgers did not dig gaps too big at the foot of the netting.

For quite a while, the fence was perfectly satisfactory for containing the deer because we found that they would not jump it simply because the grass on the other side of the fence was greener. An inestimable advantage was that the wood was now, technically, 'enclosed' so that the deer, in law, were exactly the same

My tame roe deer didn't fear my Alsatian any more than she feared me

as sheep or other livestock. With the deer 'enclosed', we were legally entitled to shoot dogs worrying them, and poaching was now theft which would entail a heavier penalty for the owners of the dogs.

We did discover subsequently that if the deer were really panicked, they could – and sometimes did – go over the fence. So did bird-nesting local youths, but I put up a copper trip wire, fine enough to be virtually invisible, which I attached to an alarm gun loaded with a 12-bore blank cartridge. Judging by the torn shreds of trousers we found on the barbed wire after it went off, it was pretty effective and very few percussions were needed to end the trespass. The fence was most effective as a dog-stopper too, and I managed to capture odd exceptions and send them to the police who lodged them in a dogs' home some miles away. The worry and trouble this caused the owners either persuaded them to keep their dogs in or find them new homes because, with only occasional exceptions, the nuisance has ceased.

Birch trees are rich sources of
food to woodpeckers, and a
delight to human eyes

24. WITHOUT A VIEW

When Fred had burned his lop-and-top and converted the solid branches to cash on his log round, the far forty acres, beyond Dunstal Pool Plantation and Holly Covert, looked a very large area of open rough ground. There were coppiced hazels, tiny birch seedlings, quite a lot of bracken and foxgloves, bluebells and fern and acres of stringy rough feggy grass.

Once I had cleared the scrub on the far side of the pool, I could sit at my study window and watch deer half a mile away prospecting for goodies. The rabbits hadn't recovered from myxomatosis so there were fewer rabbits than hares and, when Jess and I went up at dusk, we regularly saw hares and occasionally foxes and badgers foraging among thickets that sprouted, as if by magic, now that the overhead shade had suddenly gone.

There were quite a number of mature silver birch which had been left by the timber merchant who had only really been interested in selling oaks. I suppose Fred could have felled and logged them with his lop-and-top but, for some reason, he had left them and I heard the forester say they would knock them down to get them out of the way. I told him his whole patch looked like an untidy desert and, to my surprise, he agreed to leave the birches and plant round them, which at least left the area looking more like rough, feggy parkland than the desert I dreaded.

At first, it was difficult to see where the new trees were after the foresters

odd rabbit still survives to
in the afternoon sun

had finished planting because they were only a few inches high. Any trees which I plant, for food or cover or amenity, seem to take ages to get to any size. In contrast, the Forestry softwoods grew like Jack's beanstalk and, almost overnight, they were blotting out the view. If they'd been there when we came, we shouldn't have noticed because we should have accepted them as part of the surroundings, for you don't miss what you've never had. But we very soon found that deer were invisible two or three hundred yards away where before we had grown used to watching them.

Even worse, we had grown used to wandering where we liked, but pushing through a jungle of waist-high young trees is uncomfortable when the weather is fine and intolerable when wet. The Head Forester came to the rescue and told me that he would have no objection to my running my motorised Allen scythe between rows to make a few paths that Jess and I could use at will. An Allen scythe is fine for pottering along level verges, even if the grass is long and thick. It is a powerful vandal which chews its way through almost anything. But our young plantation was not on level ground and, what was worse, the stumps of felled trees lay in wait. Hitting a solid tree stump with the end of the cutter bar, even at a modest four miles an hour, slews the whole contraption uncontrollably. One second, a neat swath of grass and bramble is being laid gently to rest – and the next, the machine has changed course and is slicing off the tenant's cosseted young trees. 'Controlling' the antics of the unstoppable machine was not my idea of pleasure (*see also* page 82), so I limped home after an hour's struggle to drop, bruised and battered, into a hot bath, breathing curses on the makers of such machines and on the heads of all tree planters who made them necessary.

The few rides I managed to cut were at exorbitant cost of effort and temper but, because both Jess and I were then twenty years younger, we managed to tussock-hop over the rough terrain, even where I had been unable to mow. The snag there, however, was that rampaging through such thickets gave so much notice of our approach that everything dived for cover so that it was possible to wander right round the wood and see nothing but a blackbird.

After a year or two had passed, the young trees grew more than head height and their spreading branches reached across every space until any idea of tree movement or effective observation was a farce. Looking from the study or sitting-room window at the young pines behind the pool or on the far side of the first cross-ride – which was the boundary between the Forestry Commission and us – the view stopped as suddenly as if there were a solid hawthorn hedge, impassable barrier between our unwelcome tenants and ourselves.

I was once friendly with Old Sam, a rough Black Countryman who had been conspicuously successful in life and wore gold rings, with diamonds, and squired flashy blondes as outward symbols of his prosperity. When I asked one day where he was going on holiday, he said, 'Life is all holiday for me. I ain't done no work for fifteen years – but I've done one hell of a lot of *scheming!*' I didn't envy the status symbols of his success, but I resolved to take a leaf from his book – and start scheming myself.

25. SCHEMING FOR POSSESSION

The ninety-acre paradise we had chucked up everything to buy had effectively shrunk to half. The land leased to the Forestry Commission was rapidly developing into a monoculture of sterile pines, and the canopy of interwoven branches would soon grow so thick that no other vegetation could survive beneath it. The ground beneath the trees was becoming matted with acidic pine needles which neither bird nor beast enjoyed, except for deer that lay up there because it was warm and sheltered.

All that was left were the hardwoods of Holly Covert and Dunstal Pool Plantation, the few yards round Primrose Dell that I had vandalised by pulling out the seedling trees as fast as they were planted, Daffodil Lawn, and the pool and paddock by the house. The fact that we had lost all the attractions of forty acres in exchange for a miserly fiver a year set my teeth on edge.

The pipedream of regaining possession of the wood we'd never possessed because it was let when we bought it, turned into a recurrent nightmare. Old Sam would have done some 'scheming' – and so did I.

European Conservation Year, 1970, came to my rescue. The insecurity and change and competition of the age had set other minds thinking of more basic values, and 1970 had been declared a Conservation Year that was to be the start

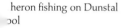

heron fishing on Dunstal
Pool

of a renaissance. Schemes were launched to concentrate the mind on conserving what was left of the countryside before it was finally ravaged by mechanisation, poisonous pesticides and the pressure of humanity trying to escape from the monstrous 'progress' it had itself created.

In one of these schemes, a Countryside Award was offered to a hundred people or organisations who were deemed to have made some 'outstanding contribution' to the countryside. Entrants were required to write a thesis explaining what they had done – and why – and the top one hundred were to be presented with a parchment scroll, signed and presented by Prince Philip, and a brass plaque, so solid that it could be screwed or bolted to something heavy enough to protect it from vandals. The organisers were nothing if not practical.

I decided to enter, to explain how I had spent the last six years, because I believed that wildlife can be managed to produce a surplus, just as pheasants have been for years. The basic difference between game and other wildlife is that surplus game is shot while other species can spill over into the surroundings where they can be enjoyed without putting the nucleus in peril.

The beauty of this scheme is that it is not necessary to start off with some fragile area of habitat threatened with destruction by the drainage of indigenous wetland, the felling of ancient woodland, poison by pesticides or destruction by the mechanical monsters of intensive husbandry. All I needed was an area of such low amenity or economic value that nobody need mind the changes I inflicted in order to encourage a wide spectrum of birds and beasts, plants and insects which would otherwise find survival difficult.

Sunlight filtering along ride edges encourages both flowers and insects

A careful survey of our wood was described which established what assets the area already contained, from persecuted herons and badgers to vandalised wildflowers, in order to decide what steps were necessary to foster them.

At the same time, the liabilities were monitored, from innocent trespass to destructive snaring, shooting and poisoning which occurred on adjacent land. Some predators, such as carrion crows and grey squirrels, were filed among the liabilities. A yardstick of the potential advantages of dynamic management was that, between 1962 and 1969, the successful heron nests had increased from fourteen to sixty-one and there seemed no reason to doubt that similar results could be achieved with other species.

Perhaps the greatest threat to the wildlife in the countryside is the conflicting interests that have to compete to enjoy their pleasure in the same small space. The interests of birdwatchers, who wished to encourage herons, and fishermen, who feared their competition, is a case in point. So one important facet of wildlife management is to foster public relations, and be harmonious enough to give and take generously so that both can survive.

I explained that herons preyed not only on trout but on perch and eels which are also predators of trout, and I did analyses of the heron food pellets which indicated a high proportion of their diet was not fish at all but rats, voles, moles and frogs so that the herons were not the threat to fishing that tradition said they were.

The local fishermen responded generously and protected their fry trout with wire netting, taking similar precautions that poultry keepers in hunting country take against foxes.

Gerald Springthorpe, the Forestry Commission wildlife warden, has always been unstinting with his help, and we culled the deer herd down to a minimum to avoid damage to neighbouring crops (*see* page 65) in the belief that it is far better to have a small herd of unharried deer than hordes of frightened fugitives which everyone regards as robbers.

Meanwhile, I disced and limed and seeded the central rides in the wood to attract the resident deer to feed away from the boundary. I discovered that, by taking pains never to get between them and what they regarded as their line of retreat when danger threatened, they grew confident enough to allow a fairly close approach.

In the thesis, I described the measures I had taken to foster insects and flowers, small birds and badgers, but my approach and the concept of SSSIs were almost diametrically opposite. An SSSI demands negative management by resistance to change, in the pious hope that what has been will remain so in the future. What truly ancient habitat has survived should obviously be preserved by protection if possible.

The 'scientific' interest of Lords Coppice, Longlands, Cockshutt Close and Ley

are loved by deer
utterflies

Wilderness, undefiled by pesticides or weed killers, fosters the widest spectrum of wildlife

Close had been stripped out by the chain-saws that felled the hardwood there. Their only value for wildlife conservation lay in what could be made of them by felling the *softwoods* in time to allow natural regeneration, introductions of species that could thrive there, and by management as positive as any modern farming technique. Holly Covert and Daffodil Lawn had been equally changed by the plough, perhaps a century and a half earlier.

But the fact that designation as an SSSI had been spurious made it no less valuable as an experiment in wildlife management because anyone, with the interests of conservation at heart, could do precisely the same in similar circumstances without putting any purists in a tizz. And, if it could be the first link in a chain of similar reserves in areas which were not otherwise of any great scientific interest, my object would be achieved.

There were 471 other entries for the award scheme, of which one hundred duly won awards. Ninety-six went to corporate bodies such as the National Coal Board for landscaping pit banks, and the Central Electricity Generating Board for making educational nature reserves. Mine was one of only four private entries to receive an award, and it was for *Investigations into Practical Methods of Wildlife Management*. It sowed the seed which helped me regain possession of the other half of our wood.

26. MORE SCHEMING

In laying out my thesis for a European Conservation Year award, I had two objectives in mind. I wanted to demonstrate, from my own practical experience and observation, that it is not necessary to own a five-star official Nature Reserve to make a significant contribution to the conservation of wildlife, so that almost any farmer or woodland owner can play his part in redressing some of the ill effects of modern pressures on the countryside. And I was determined to achieve complete mastery of my own territory, half of which was controlled – however benignly – by the Forestry Commission when I bought it.

I therefore angled my thesis so that, if the concept were accepted, it would become obvious that I could not carry on my work unless I was in a position to control the *whole* area, making what clearings among the young pines were necessary for deer 'lawns' where the beasts would be tempted to graze; sadly, this would have been to the detriment of any emergent undergrowth which would otherwise have been ideal nesting cover for small birds or concealment for hares and deer.

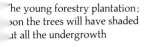

The young forestry plantation; soon the trees will have shaded out all the undergrowth

Foresters are obviously intolerant of thistles and nettles which are vital as food for a range of butterflies and moths. So when the foresters weeded their young plantation, they caused a famine which made life impossible for the insects that need such 'weeds', and 'official' disturbance by regular workers did as much harm as trespassing intruders whom the dogs had made scarce.

A weed to tidy-minded gardeners is a feast for butterflies and moths

The fact that I was one of such a small number to receive an award set the seal of authenticity on my work so again I raised the question of the surrender of my lease. This time I was lucky because the Conservator, whose responsibility it was to recommend or advise against the deal, saw that it would create no precedent. No other landowner could claim return of his land on the same grounds – because no other landowner had figured amongst those winning a Countryside Award.

My experience over many years has been that the Forestry Commission has done more towards conserving wildlife than any other government department so I knew that their sympathies were with me in spirit, even if they had to be scrupulously vigilant over the letter of the law. And my constant carping about the disturbance the workers created must have been an added inducement to the prospects of getting shot of such a nit-picking landlord!

The result was that, in 1972, the Forestry Commission surrendered my lease for the price of the young trees they had planted – which would obviously grow into money for me until I chopped them down and converted them to cash. This I was not legally entitled to do without applying for a felling licence, to clear-fell or thin, to the Forestry Commission who might not grant it until the trees were ripe – several, or many years ahead.

Although I was overjoyed at regaining autonomy over my wood, the fact that I had had to stump up £3000 concentrated my mind on the economics of the project. I don't like shelling out hard-earned money with no visible prospect of return, even for the luxury of at last being cock of my own midden. So I discussed the matter with my accountant.

He explained that there are basically two methods of dealing with the finances of woodland ownership. One is to declare all expenses and set them off against the income derived from sales of wood, paying tax only on the profits. The other, known as Schedule B, amounts to treating the wood as capital. In this case, *all* costs of maintenance have to be borne by the owner but, when the time arrives to chop down the timber and sell it, no income tax will have to be paid as the sale will be treated as realisation of capital.

This is really perfectly logical because, to take an extreme case, young trees could be planted one year, and then weeded and tended for thirty years before the crop was ripe for sale. Thus, there would be a constant trickle of outgoings for thirty years, with no profit against which to write them off because no trees were sold. Then, on the thirty-first year, when maintenance costs would have shrunk to nil, the whole wood might be felled and sold at a price which would be equivalent to the cumulative profits of thirty years. This would be assessed as 'income' on the single year, with tax out of all proportion to the earnings. By treating it as capital, under Schedule B, there would be no relief against the maintenance costs – but no income tax when it was sold.

Not unnaturally, I opted for this choice – and then did some more scheming to find some means of cashing in before I was too old to feel the benefit.

The local racecourse is a famous steeplechase course and the jumps are constructed of birch twigs, so tightly packed that they look as solid as a brick wall about three or four feet thick. In reality, horses that muff their jump and pile into the fence come to no great harm because they barge a gap through the packed birch.

I discovered that the birch saplings, growing amongst the young pines, were highly saleable when they reached the height of nine or ten feet. The racecourse workers came, cut down patches where I indicated, bundled them into the size they needed to build and repair their jumps and carted them away on lorries. The cash I received for them was ploughed straight back to pay casual labour to do the donkey work I neither had the stomach nor ability to do.

Gaining full possession of the wood – with no strings attached except that, because it was an SSSI, I was supposed to inform the Nature Conservancy Council of major management changes – altered my whole conception of the project. I was no longer satisfied with the escapist relief of leaving my job in industry to savour the joys of the simple life. Nor did I find the challenge of managing wildlife – to provide a surplus of threatened species, at whatever cost – to be totally fulfilling.

It suddenly dawned on me that, if I could make the exercise financially self supporting, it might be possible to persuade amateur naturalists, like myself, that they could make a significant contribution to conservation by creating small sanctuaries, often in unlikely surroundings. No longer would it be necessary to kow-tow to rarity or own recognised habitat that had not changed for centuries. Here was the chance for ordinary chaps to improve the lot of wildlife, simply by managing their own, ordinary surroundings and encouraging wildlife to settle there. Nor need the exercise be prohibitively expensive because, with a little native cunning, it should be possible to make the experiment pay for itself. Mine had to be cost-effective.

If enough people could be fired with enthusiasm for such activity, rarities might still be rare, but there would also be a far better chance for a whole variety of species that may be widespread now but will be gravely threatened if we squander our resources on rarity at the expense of less imperilled wildlife.

Birch is a weed to foresters, but a thing of beauty to country lovers

27. WOOD FROM TREES

One reason for getting control of the softwoods was to see precisely what went on there, so the first job was to cut some woodland rides to open up the view and give us room to get around. The obvious strategy was to cut rides radially, pointing at my study window so that, when I was seated at my desk, I would be in the key position to monitor movement in the wood.

This was more easily said than done. Clever surveyors with sophisticated gadgets would find it child's play to chop down lines of trees so that the ride they made would emerge precisely where they wanted it. We found it almost impossible! Sitting at my desk, I shuffled a six-inch Ordnance Survey map round until the compass magnetic north coincided with the magnetic north on the map. I wanted the main new ride to go diagonally through the wood, to emerge a thousand yards away, immediately above the pool in Primrose Dell. Having lined up map and compass, I took the bearing as I had been trained to do in the OTC at school, and set off on a fixed line for my objective.

The snag is that it is impossible to walk straight through a wood without making limitless diversions to step round tree trunks that get in the way. Once having stepped round a tree, the integrity of the predetermined route has been corrupted. When this has happened several times, all pretence at accuracy has been dissipated and one can emerge anything up to fifty yards or more from the original target. As a scout in jungle warfare, I should soon have ended up feet first on a stretcher for the attention of the padre.

Many trials – and endless errors – evolved a technique that was fairly satisfactory but dreadfully slow. I set off with my compass, marking the trees that seemed to be about the centre of the ride-to-be by chipping off a chunk of bark with an axe. After about fifty yards' penetration into the wood, I marked the centre tree selected for felling very clearly on opposite sides so I could find it again. As dusk was falling, I returned to that exact tree and looked back through the trees at chinks of light shining through from the lighted windows of the Lodge.

This was far more accurate than blundering round with a compass and, when I got far enough into the wood for the cluster of trunks to blot out the light, I marked what trees I thought must come down and returned next day to fell a minimum with a chain-saw.

Gradually, over sequential evenings and working away from the house, I marked a narrow swath of trees and came next day to fell them until, at last, there was a chink of light to be seen from the far end of the ride. All that was then necessary was to nibble away at trees on one side or other of the line we first cut until the narrow chink widened to a walkway.

Before getting too committed, I got quotations from timber merchants to confirm that the trees we felled would generate enough hard cash to hire a JCB digger to remove the roots, to pay for a lime spreader, and grass and clover seed to clothe the scars that we had cut. Some tree roots were blown up with explosives.

narrow slit between the
es, pointing at my study
ndow, will one day be
dened to a spacious
odland ride

Over a period, we cut and seeded three main rides, all pointing at the study window. New Ride goes (more or less!) as planned to within about fifty yards of the lip of Primrose Dell. Middle Ride is a wider, smoother version of the main extraction ride that bore the brunt of all the trees felled before Fred moved in for lop-and-top. And Pool Ride started where we had cleared the brash on the far side of the pool and cut a swath through the softwood plantation right up into Lords Coppice.

Virgin soil that had not been turned since it was ridge-and-furrow ploughed, probably a century and a half ago, was far too acidic for much but braken and bluebells to thrive in, as an understorey. So we limed and disc-harrowed the rides thoroughly before sowing them. A fair amount of wild white clover added to the grass seed not only increased the attraction of the grazing for the deer we wanted to encourage, but also liberated nitrogen to keep the soil in good heart.

It is extremely difficult to achieve the right balance of head of stock to graze a pasture because grass doesn't grow consistently throughout the season. In May and June, it grows many times faster than early and late in the season. Therefore,

Looking down to the wood from the high seat left by the Forestry Commission

Deer, undisturbed by our presence

if the head of stock is reduced until there is enough keep to sustain it in spring and autumn, it cannot cope with the summer crop. The obvious solution is to reduce the head of stock to a number which can be sustained during winter, when keep is shortest. This means that surplus grass, in summer, has to be removed or it will grow coarse, rank and wiry until nothing will eat it. This would result in deer seeking alternative food, and nipping out regeneration in the wood.

So I bought an old hay mowing machine at a farm sale and hitched it to my tractor. It had 'fingers' over which the blades chattered to slice the long grass in the main rides and leave it lying in tidy swaths which the sun and wind dried to hay for standby in the winter.

The snag was that the woodland floor was littered with hidden tree stumps, memorials of earlier felling. When the steel fingers of the mower collided with the solid oak, lying in wait for revenge, it was the oak which won. The mower fingers were twisted as useless as hairpins, only good for scrap, resulting in an expensive waste of time. So we only mowed the widest and clearest main rides from the comfort of the tractor seat, struggling round a total of six miles or so of little rides with the back-aching, muscle-tearing Allen scythe. It was quicker than a traditional hand scythe but certainly no less tiring!

The timing of such exhausting forays developed into a fine art because every miscalculation entailed an extra agonising all-in wrestling bout. The trick proved to be to leave the first cut until the growing grass was almost ready to seed. The sap had then run down so that the stems quickly withered into what would make unappetising hay. As it dried, the seeds shook out, fell beneath it and germinated, to thicken the growing sward. The mown turf below immediately started to grow, lifting the previous, withered crop a few inches clear of the ground so that, with luck and not too much rain, it was possible to mow again without raking the withered crop clear. The thin blade of the finger mower, set close to the ground, sizzled below the clogging hay to do another clear cut.

With cunning and good timing, this lasted the season, so that by the following spring the withered grass had softened into a mulch, which then returned to enrich the soil.

The deer loved the rides we'd made, and spent hours feeding in full view of the windows. Because the turf was soft and springy, it was possible to wander through the wood quietly enough to create no disturbance — and to spot both birds and animals before they saw us and took evasive action.

Best of all, the wildlife discovered astonishingly quickly that we left the rides only on very rare occasions for some specific purpose. Once they had established that we would pass by harmlessly, deer and other shy creatures ceased to be alarmed and, provided that we didn't stop to stare, we were able to observe them at closer quarters than I had imagined possible. But if we allowed them to catch our eye, proving that we had spotted them, they melted away into the shadows.

The great advantage of creating a maze of little paths was that we could vary our route around the wood, never going the same way consecutively, but conducting a continuous survey over the whole area.

28. GREEN FINGERS

Nothing good in life is easy, and to talk about the magic qualities of 'green fingers' is as stupid as saying that success in any other field is just a matter of luck.

The 'instant' garden we brought with us from the Cottage had already had seven long years of Jess's loving care so all we really did was to load her labours on a lorry and bring it over here. It has been improving ever since.

She hates the formality of geometric straight lines and sketches her ideal outline in the back of her mind's eye. The front of the Lodge is a stone-carved folly, with heavy oak cladding which imparts a slightly theatrical Hansel and Gretel air. It had deteriorated with neglect until the rainwashed shadows of its overhanging eaves made it rather sinister. It looked the sort of place that ghosts might haunt or where a witch might peer out from behind the studded oak front door.

The extension that we added was modern as tomorrow by contrast. Instead of stone, we used brick which we chose in as mellow a colour as we could. But an important aspect for both of us was that we should be able to watch, in comfort, what went on outside. So the little windows with fiddling leaded panes, designed, it seemed, to make all who looked out cross-eyed, were not included in our specifications for the extension. The sitting-room has three windows, $6\frac{1}{2}$ ft high, one is 12 feet wide, one 9 feet, and the third 7 feet.

I have no doubt that the locals wailed that we were ruining the old place – which was uninhabitable by modern standards anyway. But we were determined that our sitting-room should give such wide views that we were part of the wood and garden. Jess decided that the thing to do was to plant a hedge from where

The goats' heads, carved from solid stone, above the porch

the original house and extension met, to divide a relatively formal front garden from the easy curving, sloping lawn and flower beds where she wished to put the treasures we had brought with us from the Cottage.

We had a yew hedge doing a similar job at the Cottage, dividing the flower beds from the kitchen garden. It was a young yew hedge, only about two feet high, and she saw no technical snags in transplanting it. Her green fingers have more to do with excavating large clumps of soil that bring out the whole rootball intact, than with folklore that relies on luck. She lavishes her treasures with organic cowmuck from the farm, and leafmould from the wood.

To the north of the hedge, on the house side, she sowed and made a rectangular front lawn, tailing off under the oak tree by the garage, and she packed the shady part with bulbs including snowdrops and daffodils, as well as dog violets and prostrate junipers. In a year or so, the junipers each side of the front door looked as if they'd been there for generations. The drive side was edged by an oak-paling fence, fashioned by the craftsmen at the local timber yard, and the path from the garden gate to the front door was paved with grey stone slabs which may have started life in the quarry where the stone cladding of the Lodge was hewn.

The flower garden was to the south of the dividing yew hedge and her idea that the hedge should be grown high enough to meet the eaves so that it was not possible to see both the old house and the new extension from the same vantage point, worked fine. On one side of the yew hedge is the old Lodge and the geometric formality of the last century; on the other side, the flower garden snakes away in gentle curves to where the modern extension merges unobtrusively.

She plants flowers and shrubs for their colour and aroma and she won't have a rose that isn't sweet-scented. Many of her plants have personal associations, because all good gardeners delight in giving each other plants that have given them most pleasure. Huge clumps of rhododendron, ostensibly planted as wind-breaks and solid backdrop as well as for colour, thrive because our acid soil exactly suits their palate. Sweet-scented ponticum azaleas and viburnums add magic to the roses on warm early summer evenings; there are lilies-of-the-valley and dian-thus in profusion, and mahonia for the winter colour.

But her garden is not only for her pleasure. Jess plants sedums and michaelmas daisies as much for bees and butterflies as for the vista they provide, and the unbroken stretch of curving lawn is edged with shrubs chosen for the cover that they give to nesting birds.

A youngster who set up as a freelance gardener persuaded Jess to let him construct a rockery. He promised to get her large rocks, between half a ton and a ton apiece, and I was interested to see how he was going to tempt them into place. It would be impossible to wangle them through the two wicket gates which connect the front garden to the drive, and the ha-ha between the paddock and the garden, put there to keep the deer from raiding her precious roses, was $5\frac{1}{2}$ feet deep and 10 feet wide. The young man arrived with a Land-Rover and lowload trailer, made a temporary bridge across the ha-ha with massive timber baulks, and inched the great rocks into position using crowbars and rollers as skilfully

is never happier than when
is working in the garden.
ERLEAF) She loves sweet-
ted ponticum azaleas (TOP
) and grows sedums
TOM LEFT) not so much for
ration as for bait for
erflies. She designed the
en in seductive curves
se she hates formality

Slow worms appeared, as if by magic, in the rockery

as the chaps who built Stonehenge. When he had done, the great rocks lay casually haphazard, as if they'd been there before the Forest of Needwood, and Jess set to and made a heather garden.

She chose a wide variety of heathers so that there are always some in flower and the bees and butterflies give movement and colour whenever the weather suits them. A few years ago, we added a sunroom on the garden side of the house, which we reckon gives another month of pleasure each end of the summer season. It is often too hot for comfort from June to August but is a lovely vantage point in April and October.

We had a pleasant surprise there one morning last summer when we noticed what looked like a shining copper necklace on the grass at the edge of the rockery. Closer inspection revealed that, far from being inanimate, the necklace was a glistening slow-worm basking in the sun. Although slow-worms are really a species of lizard whose legs have not developed, it is no use denying that they *look* like small snakes, ten or twelve inches long, and some women are a bit narrow-minded about having wild snakes in the garden.

Not so Jess. She was as pleased as I was with the visitor so I begged a few young ones from a Forestry warden who breeds them in captivity. He has found that, in suitable habitat, slow-worms will choose to lie under corrugated iron sheets, placed in sunny spots in the forest, so I put a sheet at the bottom of the ha-ha, with a few young slow-worms under it, and I put the rest on the rockery which our wild visitor obviously found to his liking.

Now we are looking forward, next year, not only to the riot of colour and scent outside the windows but, with luck, to a few slow-worms adding variety and movement to the heathers on the rockery.

29. WET SETT

The artificial badger setts we had dug at the top of the bank, sloping down to Primrose Dell, worked like a charm – in summer. I had dug one sett – or caused it to be dug by a mechanical digger – on the classical lines used by fox hunters for their quarry down the centuries (*see* page 61). It had everything. The den was lined with railway sleepers to keep it warm and dry, and the horseshoe tunnel entrance, constructed from earthenware pipes nine inches in diameter, sloped gently down along the bottom of a trench, designed so that any rain that seeped in, before the covering of soil and sods consolidated, would drain away from the sleeping chamber. I put an old tree root over each entrance, partly for concealment and partly as a weather shield. It was a model sett and I am sure that knowledgeable fox hunters would have given their approval.

About ten yards away, there was another artificial earth, constructed far more simply. It was a joint effort by the Upper VI form girls, from the boarding school in the village, and senior boys from a public school, a few miles away, who had begged permission to make a sett themselves where they could come badger-watching as the fruit of their labours.

I mentioned in *My Beloved Wilderness* that the whole activity would have formed the basis for an interesting study in behaviour of *Homo sapiens* just before reaching maturity. The females of the species seem to develop first: the girls tackled the task with conscientious enthusiasm, though their results were slow (but sure) owing to the fact that their brawn was inferior to their brain. A couple of the lads showed their inverted assets by sweating blood to shower the largest clods from the trench, presumably as an instinctive display of muscle to impress

ce Deakin puts a
phone into one of the
ial earths

A muddy entrance to the wet sett

potential mates. The other lads thought it was all rather beneath them, and leaned on their shovels in rehearsal for their hopes for future life.

The result was a shallow little den, covered by no more than a foot of soil, with piped entrances which looked too short to provide any sense of security. Fox hunters, I felt, would have smirked behind their hands. Being marginally more charitable, I wished them luck, but without much conviction.

How did the mighty fall! The site at Primrose Dell was obviously well chosen because habitat, food and seclusion were beyond criticism. The only snag was that the soil was cold and puggy clay, less comfortable than warm and well-drained sand. The expensive artificial sett had been purpose-designed to counteract this weakness. Sod's Law decrees that what can go wrong will do so, and the rival setts soon proved the point. Bracken bedding, scratched to the entrance of the girls' sett (the boys' contribution being minimal), indicated that badgers had furnished it and settled in to live there. There was no sign of activity outside my monument to modern engineering skills.

After a while, the badgers obviously took a second viewing and liked what they found. Bedding was crammed into the entrance pipes of my sett, so I inserted a microphone down a small ventilation shaft built in to keep a current of air passing through the den. In due course, when I plugged in earphones to the other end of the lead, fifty yards away, I could hear the amplified snores not of one badger but of two.

Such minor triumphs of wildlife management are very sweet. It is great fun to watch birds feeding from the bird-table outside the window, or clinging to the fat or nut basket suspended from a nearby tree. It is even greater fun when tits or redstarts, flycatchers or nuthatches accept the tenancy of a bird box, made and sited with infinite care. But when wild badgers forsake their natural sett in favour of an artificial modern residence, with more than its natural share of mod cons, it feels like some achievement.

When work allows, I go out into the wood at least four times a day. The first is before or after breakfast, depending on the time the sun gets up. Jess usually comes with me after lunch and often after tea, and I go again, ostensibly to take the dogs out before we settle for bed.

On at least one of these excursions, I made a point of checking that the badgers were still in my artificial sett. Eavesdropping on the built-in mike quickly confirmed if it was tenanted or not. Badgers are very fickle creatures and, except in very large setts where they bring out old bedding to air or be replaced by new, they leave a sett altogether, often for weeks on end, to air and to allow time to become deparasitised. So, when there was no evidence of recent use, I was not unduly depressed.

It took a long time for the penny to drop, but I eventually realised that they were using the Primrose Dell sett pretty constantly during the summer months but deserting it in winter.

We have had more than our fair share of anti-badger bias from noggin-headed locals. One chap callously chucked a snared badger over my neighbour's hedge as an obscene testimonial to his expertise at laying a hang in a hedge. He has now gone where such devices have to be left outside the golden gates. So I was not initially surprised by spasmodic lack of activity at the sett, merely putting it down to leaving bedding to air or to human stupidity beyond my control. The theory that the absence was seasonal and could be connected with wet weather took some time to filter through.

It is always easy to be wise after the event, but the reason was immediately obvious. Primrose Dell, marked as a marl pit on the Ordnance Survey map, is in the low north-east corner of the wood, and the ground for a couple of hundred yards of Ley Close slopes evenly down to the pool at the bottom of the dell. The soil is impervious clay which, in wet weather, feels like a soggy sponge underfoot so that it was obvious that rain, percolating down towards the pool, would make the den as damp and clammy as a jerry-built cellar. No wonder the badgers did a moonlight flit. To confirm my suspicions, I took the cover off the den and, sure enough, the residual bedding was as musty and fusty as a mouldering grave.

Next time I needed the JCB to put stone onto a daggly ride, I got the driver to cut a ditch from the high ground to the pool, intercepting any surface water that might otherwise have seeped into the sett.

There were no results until the original dampness had been dried out by the summer warmth but, thereafter, the new ditch, which was cut below the level of the sett, drained off all moisture straight into the pool and left the sett as dry as a chip.

The badgers showed their appreciation by staying there until, well out of the breeding season, I disturbed them temporarily again. My sett was originally constructed to the standard fox-drain pattern but at this point I opened up the trench and made a foot-space between each pair of pipes. The original sett can now be used as a nucleus and badgers can get between the pipes to excavate a sophisticated sett, with a ramification of tunnels, spider-webbing for many yards. This, combined with dry conditions, has ensured continuous tenancy.

30. DEER GLADE

For some time after the Forestry Commission planted their pine trees, the young birch and bramble that grew among them made perfect fodder for the deer. The woodmen weeded it at first so that, after each weeding, the regenerating growth made helping after helping of sweet keep. After I regained possession, nobody came to weed and the young birch grew up into material for horse jumps, but the bracken stifled a large number of the seedling trees.

I was not unduly worried because I didn't want the softwoods anyway but would have needed a licence from the Forestry to clear them out and, since it was scheduled as a Site of Special Scientific Interest, the Commission would have had to confer with the Nature Conservancy Council. Relying on the whim of

The deer glade is in view of the sitting-room window

any bureaucrat for permission to do anything is bad enough. Two bureaucrats, of different departments, very often breed a bumblecrat — and dealings with bumblecrats are to be avoided like the plague.

I rather welcomed the bracken which had the effect of making a large clearing in Longlands, on the far side of Dunstal Pool, with just enough straggly pines poking up to spoil the view. I welcomed it because I have always managed my reserve with a management committee of one. Me. And my committee was of the opinion that I was perfectly entitled to 'weed' the bracken and, if there were no viable trees there was no need to apply for a licence to fell what was not there!

There were only a few scrub birch and enough sparse pines to make a few bob as Christmas trees. They were straggly and I wouldn't have found them house room myself, but the selling point is that the needles don't shed in central heating and they fetch between £2 and £3 apiece. So my management committee waited until November and then sold the trees to a contractor who cleared the site. The friendly JCB arrived and pushed out the roots, and I got out the tractor and disc-harrowed the clearing this way and that until the bracken had been shredded and destroyed. The holes where the tree roots came from were filled in by the discs and, on completion, a fairly level patch of between four and five acres stretched from the back of the pool right up to Lords Coppice.

I spread about three tons of lime to the acre and, when the March winds dried it, disced the ground again and seeded it with permanent ley and clover. It blushed a stubbly green in May and was quite good grazing by autumn.

The whole operation cost £750 and the wood fetched £800 so that we achieved a parklike deer glade, in direct view of the sitting-room windows, with £50 over towards the next project. The management committee was well pleased.

That deer glade gives us endless pleasure because it has trees on three sides which act as perfect windbreaks — and the fourth side is as open to our gaze as if it were a picture on the wall. The clover is sweet as is the young grass so the deer enjoy grazing there and, when their bellies are full, they lie up on whichever edge of the wood is shielded from the wind — preferably exposed to the sun — while they happily chew their cud.

Just at the top edge of the pool there was, previously, a very steep-sided pit whose purpose eluded me. I used to think, perhaps mistakenly, that it had been an estate saw-pit. In days gone by when oaks were felled, they were cut to length on site and cleft into fencing posts and rails by driving in steel wedges. When the old estate agent told me that it took his chaps three years to fence the deer park, it was easy to understand because they had to fell the trees and fashion the posts before erection.

There were no motor-driven chain-saws in those days, so trees were felled with axes and two-man cross-cut saws. Each mighty trunk was sawn into lengths by sweating sawyers, and then the baulks were rolled over a pit where the boss-man stood on top of the timber, holding his cross-cut saw. His partner climbed down into the pit and the two men would pull the blade up and down cutting the timber into planks. The expression 'top sawyer' was more than an empty

phrase in those days, because the poor chap in the bottom of the pit not only had to work in an uncomfortable position but also to put up with the sawdust trickling down his neck and into his ears, eyes, nose and mouth if he opened it to complain!

I was not certain if the pit at the far side of the pool had really been such a saw-pit in days gone by. Some said it was too big but, whatever its origin had been, it was just the spot to dump the great piles of roots we cleared from the deer lawn. We crushed them in with a tractor and finally covered them with a layer of earth which now conspires to cloak the origin.

A space as large as the deer glade turned out to be is ideal for observation. We don't see many foxes because Andy, the keeper next door, is an artist with a snare, and is pretty hard on foxes. I hate snares myself, but Andy is so skilful that he is selective in what he catches, and I see the same muntjac deer and the same badgers working safely here for years. What foxes do give him the slip usually settle our end of the wood and we often see them hunting rabbits on the deer glade, or simply crossing it.

In an extravagant moment, to celebrate a book which did well, I once bought a pair of 16 × 60 Zeiss binoculars. Their definition is superb but the magnification is so great that they are almost impossible to hold still in the field and the image gets afflicted with the jitters. Therefore, I keep them in my study and, with my elbows spragged on my desk to form a triangle as solid as a tripod, a fox 160 yards away across the pool apparently jumps to within ten yards of the window.

The deer glade, which is still Longlands on the map, is therefore one of our greatest luxuries. As the sun is setting, the horizontal rays bathe the glade in gentle light and we can sit, in the comfort of our sitting-room, and watch the movement out there as evening falls.

There are more rabbits than there should be, because control is very difficult among the old roots hidden in the peaty leaf-mould. But England is not England for me without the humble rabbit. When my neighbours hint, politely, that *my* rabbits come out of the wood to dine on the lush grazing of their cattle pastures, or less frequent fields of corn, I have a simple answer. I apologise and point out that honours are about even because summer snowstorms of *their* thistledown float over on the prevailing wind, to the great detriment of my wife's beloved garden – which usually changes the subject without any blood being spilled.

As the light fades, the deer often begin a hair-raising game of 'Chase-me-Charlie'. One moment they will be grazing quietly and then, for no discernible reason, one will apparently take fright and panic across the glade into the wood, swerving between the trees without slackening speed at all. Most of the others – especially the fawns and yearlings – join in, so that the reckless procession dashes through the surrounding trees, seemingly hell-bent on suicide. More often than not, there is no cause for panic, and the explanation seems to be that it is an instinctive escape routine, a sort of fire drill that teaches the next generation every hazard in the wood so that, if they are ever attacked in earnest by dogs or other enemies, they can lead them such a lethal dance that the odds will be stacked against the predator.

vening game of 'Chase-
harlie' and (INSET) the deer
ay'

31. CASH TRADE

Clearing what few trees there were to make a deer glade just broke even in cash terms by the time a mechanical digger had been hired to grub out the roots, and a lime spreader to sweeten the soil to grow good grass. My work on the tractor, discing the ground, sowing the seed and rolling the peaty soil to consolidate it, was a labour of love.

But the whole philosophy of this reserve is that it *must* be financially self-supporting in order to convince others that it is possible to conserve unlikely habitat to help wildlife survive without either being rich oneself or scrounging 'grants' from the government – which may carry obligations to ask bumblecratic permission to make any change of management.

The obvious solution is to set apart a portion of the reserve to give enough commercial return to generate capital to pay for future projects.

Although the Forestry Commission is often accused of being interested in nothing but its monoculture of boring pines, it has not been my experience. They planted Lords Coppice first and left a few young, regenerated oaks which, if their public image was accurate, they would have cleared out with the other 'weeds', or unwanted growth. These young oaks had grown to about twenty feet high, but the Corsican pines around them were stifling them so badly that their life expectancy was pretty slim.

My 'cash crop' of seedling pines

My normal reaction would have been to fell and sell the pines for about five yards' radius round each oak, to give the oak enough light and room to continue its development. There is a fair sale for the top five feet of pine trees as Christmas trees, and the trunks can be sold, by weight, for making hardboard or for the lap-fencing trade or for 'rustic' fencing.

So I decided to take out a few acres of pines, which weren't very good specimens because they had never been weeded since I'd bought them back. Theoretically, I imagine, I should have applied to the Forestry Commission for a licence. A clear-fell would have been a non-starter because the trees were not technically mature enough. A licence to thin would probably have been granted – and 'thinning' is a pretty subjective term!

However, since there seemed to be no possible grounds for argument, and since I also reckoned it would be foolish to trail my coat unnecessarily, I held a management committee meeting – and decided to go it alone.

I called in the contractors who had worked for me before and they left me in no doubt that the whole job was going to be extremely expensive. So I concocted a plan which was that, once the contractors had felled the Forestry Commission pines, I would plant new pines amongst the young oaks which were growing from the acorns of the trees which were felled just before we arrived, and which were struggling to survive. About to spend a fortune getting rid of the existing pines, you may well wonder what I was doing replanting more!

The plan was that once the seedling pines had reached about five feet, I'd sell them as Christmas trees, and be left with a lot of superb naturally regenerated young oaks, patches of bramble, stands of self-set mountain ash and aspen – both common in the wood – and the sort of shrubby understorey that I yearned for. All this would more than be paid for by the Christmas trees.

But before any replanting could begin, I knew it would be a complete waste of money to plant the thousands of trees I needed to generate cash for further work without surrounding them with rabbit-proof netting. Since fencing the wood for deer had demonstrated that netting is diabolically expensive, I set off with a trial patch of thirty rows, with forty trees in each row, choosing the patch where the best oaks were growing.

To my delight, we did better than break even. The Christmas tree tops, and the poles which formed the rest of the tree, just covered the cost of felling, burning the lop, and surrounding the whole patch with wire netting, five feet high and with an inch and a quarter mesh. Although I reckon one only gets what one pays for, I did economise on the fence, buying only light-gauge wire netting, but we reckoned it expendable if it would last until we had sold the seedlings.

Even so, success wasn't quite so easy. Nothing worthwhile ever is! The first stand of 1200 little trees grew no faster than the undergrowth – which I wanted eventually, but not yet. So the contractors had to come back for two summers to do some laborious – and expensive – hand-weeding. Some of the much-needed cash trickled down the drain before it had been generated!

However, the trees thrived from this attention, and the experiment would be successful – if only we could slash the maintenance costs.

When they had cleared the rest of the area I wished to plant, the seedling trees we bought were not enough to cover it, so we left about half the cleared area outside the fence. The deer – and, to some extent, the rabbits – descended on it like a horde of vultures. Every seedling birch that dared to show its head was nipped off before it could develop. Young grasses and brambles suffered the same fate. By the following autumn, the unplanted patch outside the fenced area of Christmas trees was cleaner of intrusive weeds than the piece slashed into submission by the hired woodmen. So we took out several more acres of Forestry Commission pines the next autumn and the cash they brought in was enough to buy and plant many more replacement seedlings, as well as erecting a fence to protect them.

Profiting by the unorthodox experiment of 'weeding by deer', we held our hand one more season and refrained from fencing in the clear patch. By the following autumn, the whole area was ready to be fenced in and planted with little trees which needed very little subsequent weeding because they had a good enough start in life to triumph over competitors.

As a result, there are over 20,000 trees growing into cash to pay for the other projects which I have in mind. They can be cropped over several years so that first we shall take out any that are near to regenerating oaks or mountain ash or other native broad-leaved trees. After the trees, the next priority will be shrubby undergrowth of bramble or scrub for nesting birds. Either the undergrowth will stifle the Christmas trees or we could flog them while the going's good, which is the obvious solution.

When the job is done, I hope to finish up with fine stands of self-regenerated oaks and dotted among the oaks will be whatever other native broad-leaved trees decide to regenerate themselves, with thickets of bramble and other cover. As the pines are sold, we shall use the profit for, amongst other things, the purchase

This patch was left unfenced until it was 'weeded' by the deer; then it was planted with Christmas trees

Rosebay willowherb is beloved by insects, and grows well in any scrubby soil

of sweet chestnut (for which the area was once as famous as for oak), beech, sycamore and wild crab apple. The Christmas trees that buy them were paid for by the original pines we felled so they will have cost nothing. Who wants government grants and other subsidies for a labour of love that leaves the world a better place?

Having just written the above section, I took the dogs up there to catch a rabbit that had got in where a badger had breached the wire-netting defences. I hadn't gone ten yards when a long-billed russet woodcock got up and snaked away, twisting and turning to avoid the shot I wouldn't have fired at him for all the tea in China. A few yards later another flushed, and another and another. Six in all got up, which is a most uncommon number so close together. A famous sherry firm used to offer a case of expensive sherry to whoever scored a 'right and left', that is, shooting a brace with consecutive shots, and as vintners are not famous for their generosity, it is a fair assumption that *six* together was indeed a bonus. It was great encouragement to know that the Christmas tree project had started on the right foot.

32. UNARMED COMBAT

Some years ago, as I described in *No Badgers in My Wood*, we had an unpleasant fracas with the local shoot. My neighbour Brian Dale, who owns the park, is no more interested in shooting than I am, but he is a businessman – with a capital B. His assets have to grow. He therefore lets the 1000-acre Bagot's Wood, which is my boundary on the west, and his 1000-acre farm, which is my boundary on the north, to a syndicate of shooters. (I use the term deliberately.)

The first lot who came were a rumbustious lot of farmers with whom I got on fine. They didn't have a keeper and turned up in an army, about twenty strong; half of them acted as beaters on the first drive, herding anything they could towards their waiting fellows. They reversed roles on alternate drives, first acting as beaters and then as guns. If it moved they shot it, and if nothing moved they were not above snatching the hat off their neighbour's head, spinning it aloft and taking a potshot through the crown. But they did predators no harm unless they were rash enough to get involved in a drive when they could count on their come-uppance. I would have wanted danger money to go out with such enthusiasts.

When that bunch moved to coverts new, they were replaced by a gaggle of Flash Harrys, out to impress the world with their success. E-type Jags and Range-Rovers were the norm, while subsidiary ciphers included custom-built guns and professionally-trained retrievers.

All that was harmless enough, but they also employed a keeper who proclaimed that he was a 'good vermin catcher' and that 'he would not tolerate a badger on his beat'. Badgers are delightful creatures – in my eyes, if not in the keeper's – but they cannot read maps or decipher shoot boundaries. When the badgers on the shoot's territory were decimated, it left attractive habitat unoccupied so I assume the badgers on my land moved over and filled the vacancy.

One of the worst aspects of the Ministry of Agriculture's extermination campaign against badgers living near to farms where cattle have TB is that, when the resident badgers are killed, whether innocent or guilty, they are inevitably replaced by badgers from the surrounding district. A successful extermination campaign in even quite a small area milks a huge surrounding area as victim after victim is replaced by his fellows from further afield.

When my badgers disappeared I assumed, rightly or wrongly, that the local keeper had trapped them, so the syndicate's boss and I had a meeting. It was not very civilised. When he refused to instruct his keeper to do anything that might result in less pheasants in the bag – in this case, to forbid him to snare or poison badgers – I said that if he would not comply, I would have more of his pheasants, legally, than all the badgers and foxes did.

Harsh words grew into deeds and I enticed his birds into my wood, which was not difficult since it is the only source of acorns in the district. As wild birds belong to whoever owns the land they're on, they were legally mine, and I shot them, trapped them, and drove them on over to more friendly neighbours' land

If the keeper did not comply, I threatened an even worse fate to his pheasants than his foxes had inflicted

Andy keeps his pheasants where he wants them by feeding 'home' rides

until I had milked our end of the shoot completely dry. The syndicate departed in search of friendlier climes a year before their lease expired, and Brian Dale advertised it to let again.

That whole episode was thoroughly unpleasant and an example of what can happen when rural neighbours fall out.

When the next lease was due to be drawn up, I was invited to the meeting because Brian Dale said that it was only fair that his new tenants should know what could lie ahead. I explained that, although passionately fond of wildlife, I was not antagonistic to genuine sportsmen. I would see they had no trespassers at our end of their shoot – and I certainly would not harm their game so long as they respected the badgers and hawks and owls which lived in my wood.

The sort of brash townies who only shoot because they think it will prove that they've 'arrived' may not realise it, but the fact is that traditional vermin do far less harm to game now than they did in days gone by. This is because immature birds, hatched in incubators and reared in protected brooders, are not exposed to the dangers of predation. By the time they are loosed in the wood, they are old enough to take care of themselves against almost any danger but cats, foxes – and men with guns.

The upshot was that, for the last five or six years, we've got on fine. When the keeper who arrived with the new syndicate retired, he was replaced by young Andy with whom I developed a mutual trust and respect. He is an absolutely honest, hard-working, first-class keeper, just the sort I would employ myself if I were interested in shooting. I never touched a pheasant, even in my wood, until the season was over, and he had my full permission to come when he liked, to 'dog' his poults back to the release pen if they strayed before the season started. On shooting days, he was welcome to bring beaters into the wood and drive the birds back over the guns waiting on his side of the boundary, though it was a privilege he rarely took and never abused.

When the season was over, I cage-trapped intensively, put the cocks in my deep-freeze and gave him the hens for his laying pen. In exchange, he was scrupulous about not harming my predators, and the proof of the pudding is that badgers bred in the House Sett, a hundred yards from my window (*see* page 136), soon after he settled in. It was a perfect example of the sort of relationship which can be fostered, even between diametrically opposed interests, so long as there is sensible give and take.

The snag is that all good things must end and shooting syndicates are volatile bodies, forever changing as old members come unstuck and newcomers make a bit of brass and can afford a status symbol. The boss of Andy's syndicate died and I've never discovered who took over for he has not so far called on his neighbours. Andy did not like the change so has moved on to a very respectable shoot where I trust he will be more happy — but the future of my badgers is, once more, in the balance.

This is not as unpredictable as it might have been. The initial experience drove home the lesson that life can be hard so I took precautions to see that it would, if necessary, be harder for others than it would for me!

I decided to make Holly Covert the best potential game cover in the area so that all the birds this end of my neighbour's shoot would naturally migrate to it. The fringe benefit is that habitat that is congenial to game is equally attractive to other wildlife. It will be my pleasure to give a friendly keeper precisely the same co-operation that Andy and I enjoyed, but if he plays it rough, as the first chap did, I shall be in a position once more to milk every bird in the area so that he will find it doesn't pay.

The first thing I did was to put in several hundred rhododendrons. They are common in game covers but frowned on by the purists because they are foreign and invasive. So are many human introductions, but those who complain of that are labelled racists.

The first rhododendrons arrived in a truck from a kind NCC man who had been thinning them out from an official Nature Reserve a few miles away. He sympathised with my desire to be able to play a trump card if any new keepers badgered my badgers — and he agreed with me that the thickets would also be enjoyed by roosting thrushes and fieldfares as well as deer. Subsequent visitors from the same department, more orthodox though of junior rank, threw up their hands in horror but, despite this, I have also made a similar shrubbery in Dunstal Pool Plantation, so *caveat* ambitious keepers!

oung rhododendrons which ill, one day, be superb olding cover for pheasants

33. NATURE'S WOODMEN

I have described, in previous books, how we have used pigs to root up the soil and leave a beautiful, well-mucked tilth as a seedbed for woodland regeneration. Seeds which fall on a thick pad of feggy grass or peat germinate and throw down roots, but the first dry spell desiccates and kills them. Acorn-seeking pigs eat most they find, but press a few deep into the soft soil with their sharp little hooves, and tiny oak trees, bramble and scrub spring up in the bare soil they have excavated. Three quarters of Holly Covert is predominantly oak and one quarter is birch – but the understorey is very bare because all regeneration was nipped out by the Bagot goats. Even when the goats had gone, any broad-leaved seedling bold enough to raise succulent leaves above ground level was promptly nipped off by the deer, and the only remedy was to get such a thriving crop that the deer could not eat it as fast as it grew. The alternative, of course, was to cut down the size of the deer herd to small enough numbers to have no significant effect on the vegetation, and this I was not willing to do. In any case, it would have been impossible to 'cultivate' Holly Covert using pigs without taking steps to prevent them straying to areas where they were not wanted – such as the paddock by the house or the sward of Daffodil Lawn. The drive side of Holly Covert was already fenced to keep the deer in and hounds out, and it was fenced off from Daffodil Lawn to keep domestic stock, grazing there, from getting into the wood where they might have eaten poisonous rhododendrons.

We therefore fenced the ride between Holly Covert and Cockshutt Close with sheep netting, adequate to contain the pigs but cheaper than the netting round the boundary. It was also adequate to exclude the deer – until it aged and perished, by which time I hope that there will be more regenerated undergrowth than the deer will destroy.

As well as encouraging natural regeneration where the pigs have rooted, I take the opportunity to plant any native trees that come my way in this fenced deer-proof area. Wood pigeons, blackbirds and thrushes roost in the yew trees in the paddock by the house. The birds eat holly berries as well as yew, and the kernels, cracked during digestion by the birds' gizzards, are excreted onto the leaf-mould and loam below. Nature's treatment in the birds' digestive system ensures a high percentage of germination, and there are many seedling hollies below the yews which I also transplant to Holly Covert, though it would obviously be too labour-intensive to protect so many with wire surrounds.

One satisfactory result of tenancy by the pigs is that drifts of bilberry are returning spontaneously, as well as seedling oaks – and one of the problems is that the pigs will eat them and defeat the whole object of the exercise. It is no use my asking the experts what to do because it is an unorthodox exercise, outside the experience of office-bound boffins. Their instinctive reply to anything original they have not read about is that you shouldn't be doing it anyway.

So the experiment has been – and still is – a matter of trial and error. I have established that, if pigs are paddocked in a small area I want to clear completely of bracken, for example, they kill everything green first, then they uproot and investigate what lies beneath and finally sift through the soil until it is a fine tilth. If any small tree or plant is enclosed in such an area, that will be the end of it.

Therefore, it becomes a matter of nice judgement when to open up the pigs' enclosure and loose them into the whole thirty acres, to wander where they will and turn over random patches to provide the desired result. If they get in too soon and any cherished introduction happens to be toothsome – they will eat it! So we don't give them their freedom until the acorns start to fall; then they range widely, searching for the acorns and fallen berries rather than digging for less obvious gold or eating forbidden fruits which I have introduced.

If the timing is right, they do a wonderful job. When they are cleaning up the crop of fallen acorns, they start to turn over odd, apparently haphazard patches of only a few square yards. This is precisely what I want because they leave a random mosaic of disturbed soil which is ideal for seedlings to take root in.

I have tried, in vain, to establish just what they choose to dig next, and have stood within a yard or so without finding a solution. They smack their lips and make a great many uncouth but satisfied noises. They certainly eat all acorns and fallen crab apples, snails and beetles that happen to come their way – but I am no wiser now about what they are looking for as opposed to finding accidentally.

Right down the centre of Holly Covert is the main ditch that feeds the pool.

Previous tenants of Holly
Covert, the Bagot goats

In the autumn, when the acorns fall, the pigs run free in Holly Covert

It is about ten feet across the top and at least six feet deep, with steep, straight-cut sides. Pessimists warned that the pigs would fall into it and might be damaged fatally, and we did discuss the possibility of guarding it with a fence, either electric or conventional, but decided that pigs, in olden days, whose owners had the commoner's right of pannage, had to take pot-luck – and so would these. Having had them in the wood for several years, experience has taught us that it was the right decision.

The great bonus has been that, by careful management in timing the stay of the pigs loose in the wood, they have opened up the surface, as we hoped, but have done very little damage, either to plants we have introduced or which have grown spontaneously – or to themselves by eating anything that didn't suit them. The only mishap (described in *No Badgers in My Wood*) was when both a pig and a fox died of poisoning. We sent the fox to the Ministry of Agriculture to have the poison analysed, but they were unco-operative, and took months to do a post mortem which never isolated what poison killed them, and left us none the wiser.

I admit that I do get irritated when they desecrate the maze of little rides that I keep clear with the chain-swipe behind the tractor so we can get about easily, while not creating any disturbance. When the rides have been cut two or three times, a more succulent sward develops than the feggy, untamed surface of the rest of the wood. The pigs begin by grazing this, just as they do the grass which grows in conventional farming country. But God did not equip them with irresistible leathery snouts with no divine purpose, and they demonstrate precisely what this is by putting down their noses and ploughing furrows across and up and down the woodland rides. In due course, when they have cleaned up the wood as they were set to do, I have no conscience about despatching them to the butcher so that I can restore the surface of my rides and eat home-cured ham for breakfast.

34. PARTNERSHIP

Among my greatest pleasures is the fact that my job as a professional rural journalist brings me into close contact with some of the best naturalists in the land. I owe much of my knowledge and the introductions to some of my most valued friends to the late Miss Frances Pitt.

She was of the old school of practical field naturalists, a remarkable woman who farmed 600 acres, not with a farm manager but with a working foreman so that she made all the key decisions herself. She was a Master of the Wheatland Hounds — which were a highly respected pack in her day — and she wrote many books and contributed regularly to national magazines and papers. She illustrated her own work and was reputed to have taken over 10,000 wildlife photographs.

Miss Pitt was in the habit of throwing famous Sunday luncheon parties to which guests were summoned — not invited! And we always went, in the certainty that fellow guests would be stimulating and distinguished in their field. She 'collected' artists and huntsmen, writers and landowners, and specialists in all sorts of rural fields — but never academic scientists or bureaucrats for whom she had no time.

It is common, in life, to have a magnum of interesting acquaintances but he is a lucky man who can count more than a handful of such friends.

Gerald Springthorpe has been one of my closest friends for more than thirty years and I know no better practical naturalist nor more knowledgeable country-

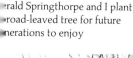

Gerald Springthorpe and I plant a broad-leaved tree for future generations to enjoy

A swinging flap, let into a fence where badgers normally cross, will be accepted by them but will keep out rabbits

man. His job is Wildlife Officer to the Forestry Commission and, although he lives only a few miles away, he has an enormous parish and travels widely in forests from the Lake District, along the Welsh Border, down to the West Country.

Gerald's deepest love is deer, especially fallow deer. He eats, drinks and dreams them. He never went to university but he has forgotten more about fallow deer than most of the specialist boffins will ever know.

We see as much of each other as we can, and he comes over to go round the wood, sometimes two or three hours before eight o'clock breakfast, or as evening is drawing in when he has finished work. We go into the wood almost every Saturday or Sunday morning and we always discuss in detail the current projects that I have in mind. We don't always agree, especially on deer, because he would prod me to allow as many in the wood as it will possibly hold. I know that we should have a far better and thicker shrub layer if it weren't for the fact that we have too many deer already!

He gets a lot of trouble, in State-owned forests, from louts with terriers, digging for badgers, and he has tried all sorts of ruses to defeat them. When trees have been felled, the heavy roots are often pushed out by powerful tractors to make subsequent cultivation easier. He arranges with the forester to have piles of these roots pushed on top of badger setts, burying them beneath debris too heavy to move by hand. The badgers simply dig out — or in — around the roots but the tunnels beneath are inaccessible and quite impossible to dig by hand with spades.

Gerald and I plan how we can increase the network of little rides in my wood without having to fell trees to make way for them; we also introduce new hardwood trees and shrubs. We plan where to site new artificial setts, to attract badgers from hazardous areas and to tempt them to stay, and he has introduced me to people who have helped to establish many of the creatures which have settled here — such as the woman who gave me a roe deer, or the chap who brought me a bag of grass snakes and slow worms.

My neighbour's wood, over the drive, is still let to the Forestry Commission, and the wildlife there is under Gerald's charge. He has persuaded high echelons of officialdom to allow him to make clearings where rare flowers grew before the softwood trees arrived. He is currently in the process of back-filling a drainage system which was put in to drain an ancient moss so that a few more pines could grow. When he has finished, the ground will revert to its original wet state so that species lost for a few shillings' worth of pit props will get a new lease of life. He has reptile areas, and spots managed in the interests of butterflies and flowers. Badger setts are sacrosanct and there are nesting-boxes in which birds and bats can thrive. For the price of a few commercial trees, he and those like him have won a reputation for the Forestry Commission that is second to none in the field of conservation.

When the Commission has improved the quality of habitat until it is of vital importance for wildlife, the Nature Conservancy rightly designates it as a Site of Special Scientific Interest, which by then it is, and claims the right to be con-

A 'creep' through the fence to
let straying muntjac back into
the wood

sulted about its future management. It must be pretty galling to lose control and credit just when the job has entered Easy Street.

One man's loss is another's profit — and I have learned a great deal by going out with Gerald to share the experience he has gained by trying similar experiments in wildlife management to mine — except on a grander scale. And perhaps he scores too, because if he has an idea that even the top brass of the Commission think a bit way-out, we can try it here, where only a committee of one can veto it!

Badger gates, which are swinging doors in wire-netting fencing, have been standard practice for woodmen for many years. Until the end of the last war, badgers were counted as vermin because, when an area was fenced with small mesh netting, to exclude rabbits from young trees, it was common for badgers to burrow under the fence in order to reach their traditional feeding grounds, and the rabbits, of course, got in through the gap the badgers had made.

Gerald joined the wildlife section of the Commission on the ground floor when Herbert Fooks, a distinguished figure in wildlife conservation, had just been charged with the task of cleaning up the Commission's image. Destroying badgers as vermin because they let rabbits into young plantations was one of the main causes of justifiable public criticism. So badger gates were constructed and erected where fences blocked off the traditional runs that badgers had used for generations. They found it far easier to shove the swinging flap aside than to dig a fresh hole under the fence, and took to them almost as easily as a cat takes to a cat-flap fixed in the back door of a house.

I had great difficulty with badgers digging under the deer fence and letting out the young of a pair of muntjac deer I had hand-reared a year or so before. We put in badger flaps, designed and sited by Gerald, but, though the badgers used them, the fence was so long that they occasionally opened up another gap I didn't find for a week or so. If the muntjac found it first, they got out and often failed to find the way in again, so wandered forlornly up and down outside the fence — in possible danger from my neighbours who might snare them in fox wires, or dogs which might worry them.

So Gerald and I put our heads together and designed a funnel entrance at the top of the hedge bank, so constructed that anything popping through it had to jump down across the ditch into the wood on my side. It was almost impossible to return the same way because the small end of the funnel was too high above normal ground level for easy entry — so muntjac patrolling the outside of the fence had an easy one-way passage in, but couldn't find the exit. It worked on the same principle as medieval deer leaps by which the aristocracy were licensed to stock their deer parks from adjacent forest to ensure a constant supply of fresh venison before the days of ice-houses and fridges.

Gerald and I have piled up old tree roots, as the Normans did, to encourage rabbits to take up residence just where we want them so that we can catch them in cage traps when they sally forth to feed.

Ours is a partnership of innovation and experiment in wildlife management where we aim to help wildlife in the general countryside as well as in the remote spots that only scientists find interesting.

35. THE HOUSE SETT

Having persuaded badgers to settle in the inhospitable clammy clay at Primrose Dell, it was vital to offer alternative accommodation. They are not such inveterate wanderers as otters are because they live in colonies, or social groups, and settle in smaller territories which they defend implacably.

Some badger setts are centuries old, with tunnels interlinked over hundreds of square yards, usually in wooded hillsides. These setts are continuously occupied except when the animals are disturbed or persecuted, but they are so large that the badgers need occupy only one portion at a time, and then move to another section when the first becomes parasitised or otherwise untenable.

Where food is too scarce to support a large community or, as in my area, where illegal action is taken against them, badgers often occupy smaller setts for a period, then desert them, only to return again when they have had time to deparasitise and air — for badgers are natural prey to fleas and ticks, but scrupulous in hygiene.

I wanted the artificial sett at Primrose Dell to provide maximum, not minimum, security, so when we noticed the badgers were not in residence, we improved

The badgers took to a pile of roots in order to make their own sett within eighty yards of the house

it by opening up the trench which buried the pipes and leaving a gap between each pair of adjacent pipes, as described on page 115.

The very fact that we were able to make alterations in their absence was eloquent testimony that they did not occupy it continuously – and when they left it, they must have holed up on my neighbours' land because there wasn't another sett on mine.

That was the reason why I wanted to give them an alternative and, at the same time, I decided to chance my luck and try to persuade them to settle near to the house instead of in the remotest corner of the wood.

There is an ancient, sprawling rhododendron at the edge of the wood, about eighty yards from the study and sitting-room windows. The Middle Ride runs along the south side of Dunstal Pool Plantation, on one side of the rhododendron, and the New Ride is cut radially to the study window on the other side. If I could persuade badgers to take up residence behind the rhododendron clump, we should see them cross one or other ride each time they emerged to forage in daylight.

I didn't want to make another conventional 'artificial drain' as Gerald and I planned to experiment with other ways of frustrating the efforts of prospective badger diggers.

Next time the JCB was in the area, I got him to bulldoze a pile of old tree roots I had already collected with the tractor. We also put two tree trunks, parallel and about a foot apart, leading from the centre of what we hoped the badgers would regard as home, to the edge of the prospective sett. We chucked a few tree roots on top of the trunks to prevent the channel they formed filling up with earth, and then covered the whole lot with soil excavated from the bank of the ditch which ran nearby to fill Dunstal Pool.

When we had finished, there was a mound of soil about ten feet high and ten yards across, with a fair number of gnarled tree roots buried at random in the pile. The theory was that, with minimum excavation, badgers could creep between the two tree trunks to the centre of the pile. Once there, they could excavate internally, to make warm, dry dens – or 'overns' as the experts call them – under the buried tree roots.

Wildlife is never in a hurry, and nothing happened for several months. Then the rabbits reckoned that the wet soil piled on by the JCB had dried out enough for them to do a trial dig. They found the tree roots and made the simple single tunnels – or 'stops' – where they drop their young. This attracted foxes which dug out a few of the rabbit nests, then decided the whole pile was a pretty desirable residence and inhabited it, though only in foul weather, not for breeding purposes.

I only inspected the mound once a week in order to avoid the least risk of disturbance – and one day was rewarded by obvious evidence which indicated interest by badgers. Outside the main entrance formed by the parallel tree trunks we had laid as the foundation, there was a pile of freshly excavated soil, enough to have filled a wheelbarrow. The five-toed footprints of a large badger were clearly visible.

Greatly excited, I couldn't resist making daily inspections after that, though

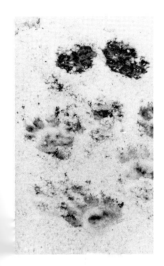

A badger paw print in the snow

RIGHT The badgers left a trail of snow, leaving wisps of bedding behind

I left the dogs behind and stopped five yards away and examined the evidence through my binoculars. After a time, there was no sign of badgers for a week or so, after which spasmodic visits indicated only that badgers were foraging there but had not yet decided to take up permanent residence.

Patience was rewarded in the end, so Gerald and I erected a low observation hide, a few yards downwind, from which it was possible to get a closer look before dusk and after dawn.

A single badger, obviously an old boar, initially made his home there, possibly because he had been chucked out of a breeding sett by the sow who didn't reckon there was room for him and her cubs in a restricted space. The following season, a very small sow joined him and I took her for a previous year's cub and didn't think she was mature enough to breed. As often happens, I was wrong. She produced a brace of cubs, and Jess and I had great fun watching them, aloft in the hide or from the sitting-room, when they grew old enough to forage.

One mistake I made was to build the mound behind the rhododendron clump. I sited it there because we thought such a large pile of naked earth would be an eyesore from the house. It wasn't naked for long, of course, because I seeded it with grass to make a solid mat of root which would stop the rain percolating through. Had I sited it in full view of the house, we would only have had to have suffered the earth pile for a season, yet we could have watched in comfort nightly, instead of making a special effort to go up to the hide — where we were eaten alive by mosquitoes.

Nevertheless, it was a major triumph, by my standards, to persuade wild badgers to settle of their own free will and where the clay soil is anything but ideal — and, most of all, within spitting distance of the windows. They have now dug out such huge mounds of soil that I am seriously worried that the hollowing shell will collapse, and thus drive them elsewhere. So I plan, when I make a bit of easy money from the Christmas trees, to hire the JCB again and build a Mark II version, correcting the faults I see in hindsight.

Lady's smock loves wet ground
and green-veined white
butterflies love lady's smock

I shall site it in the open on the other side of New Ride and lay a few inches of limestone chippings as a base before introducing roots and covering them with soil, again from along the side of the deep ditch that feeds Dunstal Pool. We shall need so much of this soil that it will leave a shallow hole of, perhaps, half an acre – and this, in times of flood, will silt up and leave a lovely wetland with lady's smocks and marsh marigolds to fill Jess's eyes with pleasure, and be a breeding ground for succulent slugs which will give equal delight to the badgers. I have already fixed a floodlight in the trees so we can watch the badgers feed when dark has fallen; they do not appear to notice it. Observing them colonising another sett will be something to look forward to.

36. RELICS OF ANTIQUITY

Although signs of ancient ridge-and-furrow ploughing on Daffodil Lawn and in Holly Covert were obvious proof that this area of Needwood Forest was anything but untouched by the hand of man, there were still plenty of survivors from ancient woodland.

Two trees in the fringe of woodland that borders Daffodil Lawn were unknown to me – but there is nothing strange in that because I am a most indifferent botanist. When one blew down, I took a closer look and, still being no wiser, I had it identified. It proved to be a wild service tree and a short while later I mentioned it casually to the Tree Preservation Officer of the County Council. He almost went into orbit with excitement because it was apparently the first wild service to be recorded in his parish and the survivor was – and is – a very fine specimen.

As the species is a reliable indicator of ancient forest – and our tree was a

There are still relic trees and vegetation which were part of Needwood Forest before Daffodil Lawn was cleared

specimen – the conclusion was that our soil suits it. I put a bit of sheep fence round the surviving tree so that it could throw up suckers which would not be nipped off by the sheep which graze Daffodil Lawn in summer.

The purists *hate* introductions and one dear old chap in the local natural history society had spent a lifetime mapping all the species of flower and tree which occur 'naturally' in each 20-kilometre square on a map of the county. I can quite see that introducing plants which were not there when he made his survey would make a porridge of his records. I sometimes think that such theorists would rather see a species become extinct, when its habitat is destroyed, than see it turned into what they regard as almost a 'garden' plant to be introduced wherever it will grow.

I believe that mechanisation and chemical farming are here to stay. It may be possible to soften their impact by putting planning controls to 'preserve' selected sites, or by reducing the toxicity and persistence of chemical poisons by law. But we shall never stop the clock and we have no more chance than King Canute of turning the tide of progress. The practical solution seems to me to be to transport species of plant, animal and bird which are threatened in one area to places where they can continue to thrive, even if this means moving rarities such as orchids or vulnerable trees.

Therefore, I had no scruples about fencing in my solitary wild service tree and allowing it to throw up suckers, and I also had no scruples about transplanting those suckers to Holly Covert or any other part of my wood which is hospitable enough to give them viable sanctuary.

I was comforted to discover that the Tree Preservation Officer was of a like mind. He deemed it his duty to *preserve* trees, not to stand by and watch them perish if he happened to have no official way of controlling adverse changes to the management of their environment.

He took away a bundle of suckers, to run on in his nursery, saying that he would bring back some to transplant in the parts of my wood where they would thrive. Unfortunately, he retired shortly afterwards and I never got my suckers.

There are great drifts of wood sage and wood-sorrel in Holly Covert, possibly descended from the same plants that flourished here in the days of Robin Hood. Humble honeysuckle, pale and fragrant, still grips the stems of hazels in a tight enough embrace to leave sticks with spiral patterns for walking sticks and, most optimistic sign of all, bilberry is returning to where it thrived before the Bagot goats obliterated it.

The corner of Dunstal Pool Plantation nearest the Lodge is predominantly oak, and I have fenced in half an acre to rear my annual crop of pullets which lay fresh eggs for the house. I go there every day to feed them, and I would have laid heavy odds that I could identify every tree in that patch. But I was surprised by the wild crab apple tree I found (*see* page 24) and I confess that there is not a tree in the wood I would spare if I had to choose between it and the crab. The fact that I had lived within fifty yards for almost twenty years, before discovering what my neighbour was, confirms how easy it is to overlook something just in front of one's nose. One tree I did manage to save is a lovely old hedge maple on the east of Cockshutt Close which the woodmen spared, at my request, when Fred was lop-and-topping. Along the boundary fence, there is an acid old ditch which drains into Primrose Dell, and this hedge bank and the steep sides down into the dell are a mass of giant marestail which congeals to a forest as it gets to water level. It is a queer, segmented plant, as primitive as it looks, and I was taught at school that the coal we burn in our grates was once a huge form of marestail which was compressed and fossilised, thousands of years ago. The marestail in our wood is a tenuous survivor and the fact that it still thrives is as good as an entry in the botanical equivalent of Burke's Peerage as a pedigree of continuity which will go back to the days when Needwood really was an ancient forest.

There are dog's mercury, primroses and cowslips, also the odd oxlip as evidence of the illicit mating of the two. Daffodil Lawn has the wild daffs, whose parentage I doubt, for the flamboyance of the Gothic lodge suggests its original owner may well have planted them. But I doubt he would have bothered with the drifts of common windflower or wood anemone, which make the banks so lovely in spring, or the lady's smocks, in undrained patches, or wild violets in the sward.

Something I have not yet fathomed is what controls where bracken is predominant rather than fern. Dunstal Pool Plantation and Holly Covert are liberally spattered with large clumps of fern, which thrives in summer and withers and shrinks in the first frost. Several varieties of fern thrive in the rough to the

old hedge maple grown
 seeds left by birds in days
 past

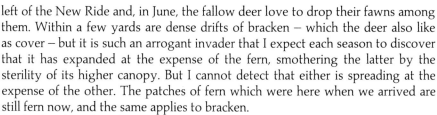

left of the New Ride and, in June, the fallow deer love to drop their fawns among them. Within a few yards are dense drifts of bracken – which the deer also like as cover – but it is such an arrogant invader that I expect each season to discover that it has expanded at the expense of the fern, smothering the latter by the sterility of its higher canopy. But I cannot detect that either is spreading at the expense of the other. The patches of fern which were here when we arrived are still fern now, and the same applies to bracken.

The bracken does have one advantage. It is very susceptible to frost and a hard frost in May will frizzle the young bracken shoots which delays growth a week or two. Whatever the weather, it comes into leaf after the bluebells bloom and the higher parts of the wood, both on the open swath to the east of Cockshutt Close and the rides that bisect it, are a carpet of blue that always takes my breath away.

The corner of Ley Close, above Primrose Dell, only has a few pines, and what there are have been climbed and strangled by dense bushes of wild rose. I thin out the trees around each rose to give it air and light, and that area is now developing into the dense type of shrubby vegetation in which it is ideal for small songbirds to nest. Although it is 500 feet above sea level, the ground around Primrose Dell is like an upland marsh; it is rich in alders, and there were lovely drifts of wild spiraea until the deer discovered that they liked it and wolfed it to extinction.

37. THE PROFITS OF PEACE

The herons are an interesting halfway house between sport and conservation. They are considered an almighty nuisance by many fishermen who cannot grasp the basic fact that, if they insist on filling streams and reservoirs with an unnaturally high density of idle, stew-fed fish, they must expect predators to congregate to feed on them as tits flock to fat on a bird table.

Our herons, whose ancestors had nested for generations in the neighbouring Bagot's Wood, were dispossessed by tree-fellers and forced to migrate over the drive to Holly Covert, which was the last remaining stand of the wood which had been their home (*see* page 30). They arrived in Holly Covert the year we bought it.

Local birdwatchers were up in arms about the trees which were being felled, and put pressure on the Nature Conservancy to prevent any more being destroyed. It is not legal to slap on a conventional Tree Preservation Order in woods licensed for felling, but when the NCC discovered that it was, in any case, my intention to protect them, they were happy enough to designate the wood as a Site of Special Scientific Interest (*see* page 186) which, in theory, might help if there was any threat to alter the use of the wood because they would have first to be consulted.

Before we came, there was already a licence which allowed the trees to be felled, so the SSSI protection was very hollow. All the NCC could do was to 'advise' against altering the character of the habitat itself which was technically of no great importance because most of the ancient wood had long since been felled and replaced by trees which were probably little more than a century old.

It made the point that is the kernel of this book. I fully concede that it is vital to protect the continuity of what small percentage of our land is ancient and has been relatively unchanged or unspoiled for generations. But I believe that it is even more important to involve the vast numbers of ordinary citizens, who have an instinctive affection for our native wildlife, but are never likely to become the possessors of exceptionally rare or 'important' habitat, in projects where they can make *personal* contributions.

When we arrived, there were fourteen herons' nests, salvaged by the birds themselves, from the traditional heronry which, at maximum, numbered forty-four. By 1985, the number had swelled to eighty, by far the largest heronry in the county, and the Nature Conservancy Council wrote to say that, from 1980 to 1985, the number of nests *averaged* sixty-nine, '*which was more than 1% of the total number of nests in the British Isles*'.

Because of this, and the daffodils, they informed me unofficially that they proposed to confirm that Goat Lodge would be 'protected' as a Site of Special Scientific Interest under the 1981 Act instead of merely 'notified' under the 1949 Act. By whatever yardstick you measure it, 1% of all the herons in the country congregating to nest in one small wood, of no importance save for their presence, is quite encouraging.

I maintain that the vital aspect is that they have *chosen* to nest here, not because there is anything intrinsically important (or 'scientifically interesting') about the habitat itself, but because they have been given seclusion and security which could have been provided by any keen amateur naturalist who controlled any small parcel of woodland to which the birds had retreated when their ancient nesting trees were felled. In other words, the validity of scheduled sites depends as much, or more, on the goodwill of the owners as it does on any artificial criterion dreamed up by bureaucrats. If government can induce landowners to become actively involved in conservation, there is every chance for the future. But if they try to shackle them with red tape, they will discover that unwilling horses only kick when flogged.

The herons sometimes – but not often – turn up to prospect for nesting sites over the Christmas holiday. If subsequent weather is foul, they disperse again, but it is their first appearance which rings the bell. We look forward to their coming and, if they fail to put in an appearance, our faces are long and we convince ourselves that they have found a better site and have deserted us. Or that chemical pesticides have poisoned the frogs which, in turn, have annihilated birds which caught them in their death throes. Such self flagellation convinces us that when our heronry is untenanted in spring, it will be an ill omen and our luck, too, will vanish. It doesn't happen though. They always *do* turn up, though often not until February.

The first arrivals bag the nests they want and sit on top of them, making their disgusting belching threats – which presumably both attract a mate and warn off rivals. The most impressive time to hear them is at dead of night when the moon is full. We waken from the depths of deep sleep to hear the most horrific squabbles in the wood and, if we forget to warn our guests, they tell hair-raising stories at breakfast about foxes fighting or killing pet cats, or – if they are really imaginative – of suspected murder and rape across the fields. It isn't foxes fighting or mating, or human victims either; it is only our feathered guests being coarse about warning off their rivals.

From the time we first hear them until the middle of May we avoid trespassing on their privacy because they are – wisely – so suspicious of humans, who are too often trigger-happy, that they beat a retreat and allow the carrion crows to rob their nests.

There are not many heronries in Staffordshire and most woodland owners prefer their birds to fishermen and are proud of being selected as exclusive hosts. So there is a bit of professional jealousy and mutual suspicion about the possibility of a little gamesmanship influencing the accuracy of counting nests!

Young Ruth Springthorpe, Gerald's youngest daughter, nominally 'helps' Jess around the house and garden. In reality, we regard her as a member of the family and she shares our chores – and our failures and successes – and we enjoy her cheerful company. Ruth and I have got the counting of nests down to a fine art. We long since learned that it is quite impossible to stand at a vantage point in the wood, look in one direction and tot up the number of nests we can see before shifting our gaze to take the roll-call of another lot. Within three minutes,

arguments break out because one thinks 'this' nest was included in 'that' group and the other is positive it wasn't.

We have found that there is only one certain route to accuracy and this is to nail a sequentially numbered plant label, including the date, to every tree which supports a heron's nest — and recording *precisely* how many nests there are. For a nest to be counted as 'successful', there must be 'whitewash' beneath it — where fledglings have excreted over the nest — or, better still, the shells of newly hatched eggs, or fledglings large enough to be seen from below.

We always do the job between May 10th and 14th (my birthday!) because most birds then have young too large to be damaged by crows when their parents are scared off. If we leave it until later, the leaves grow too dense to see the nests.

Because we are not only determined to count the nests precisely, but also to be *seen* to be accurate, we invite Frank Gribble, the local secretary of the West Midlands Bird Club, to join us as a witness and when we get a record number, as we did in 1985, we go back and celebrate with Jess in the knowledge that *we* are pleased that providing no more than a sense of security is so effective.

38. HEDGING FOR BIRDS

The boundary of Holly Covert, from Daffodil Lawn to the Lodge, is just on half a mile. It was unfenced when we came, and was frequently breached by trespassers who came into the wood to amuse themselves by heaving stones into the herons' nests, cutting hazel wands for bean or walking sticks, or digging up clumps of primroses. The goats had scoffed everything which grew low enough to reach, so, when the wood was fenced to keep deer in and foxhounds out, I decided to give the birds a bonus by supplying them with instant nesting sites.

Instead of erecting the netting fence along my boundary, which is defined on the deeds as my side of the drive, I set it about five yards into the wood, to leave a verge between fence and drive which neither my deer nor the goats could reach. And I decided to plant a hedge along this verge which would at least prove to critics of the countryside that not *everyone* is engaged in grubbing up hedges for the subsidy paid by the Ministry of Agriculture. This hedge would be the exception by being planted while other hedges perished.

It was to be no ordinary hedge, either. I decided to set a hedge of blackthorn plants which would not be to every farmer's taste because blackthorn is not as amenable as hawthorn to the discipline of laying, and it has what farmers regard as the nasty habit of throwing out suckers which allow a disciplined hedge to spread insiduously into invasive, thorny thickets.

When I went to a nurseryman to get quotations for the hedging plants, I discovered that blackthorn was four or five times as expensive as hawthorn. Cutting my coat by the cloth I could afford, I therefore ordered five hawthorn to every blackthorn – and planted a hawthorn hedge which had one blackthorn planted between every group of hawthorn. The nurseryman said that if I only trimmed it on one side, as I intended, the blackthorn would eventually sucker until it had taken over to make dense breaks of impenetrable tangled bushes.

I decided that a thorny jungle, bordering the wood, would continue to deter trespass long after my wire-netting fence had rusted and collapsed and, at the same time, the shelter of the hedge would provide protection against predators of birds which could not survive in the present open habitat.

The top two hundred yards, where Daffodil Lawn is bordered by the drive, more than came up to expectations. The hawthorns grew like willows and when they had grown to about ten feet high, I was able to get Fred to lay them into a neat, old-fashioned hedge.

The spacing of the blackthorn proved about right for it suckered along the hedgebank bordering onto Daffodil Lawn just as the nurseryman had predicted. In addition, my neighbour's Great Lawn faces Daffodil Lawn across the drive and since there are no large trees to shade the young hedge plants, they were able to get all the light they needed. The broad band of thicket along the edge of the lawn has now been laid twice by Fred and is beginning to look as stockproof as the jumping fences in good hunting country. It has also proved an effective deterrent to anyone with designs on the daffodils.

Blackthorn in full blossom: in the autumn, this provides the fruit for sloe gin. May blossom, bramble and hawthorn berries

The rest of the hedge, along the border of Holly Covert down to the Lodge, has hardly thrived at all. Although the drive is almost due north–south and catches a reasonable amount of sun each side of midday, it is rather shadowed by mature oak trees on my side, and pines ten or fifteen yards away on the edge of Big Wood.

Nobody dealing with wildlife gets far without more than a fair ration of patience, and it is not one of my deficiencies. Each spring and summer when a variety of palatable keep was available, my little hedge grew a few inches. For several years, the bracken grew faster which meant the hedge only had the chance to develop between the end of March and May. After May, thick bracken obliterated it, and in autumn the deer gave it a severe unseasonal pruning. I could have tolerated this if the vandals had been my own deer (but they were safe behind my expensive wire-net fence) but to have my labours ruined by someone else's deer, trespassing from Big Wood, was no good for my temper.

Even so, the hedge is gradually winning because it is higher than the bracken and is thriving in spite of it. Bramble, sown by blackberry seeds dropped by the birds, has colonised the strip between hedge and fence, and each year finds the hedge a little higher and thicker.

The undergrowth that has flourished between the drive and fence alongside Daffodil Lawn is now the best cover in the whole wood, and is already a favourite nesting place for birds – and I'm only sorry that it is outside the fence. One day, long after I'm gone, enquiring minds will ponder why such thick cover was planted without any obvious motive, because it is unlikely that anyone will guess that it was planted by an eccentric naturalist simply so that he could leave the world a little better place.

A few yards from the hedge, on the other side of the fence in Holly Covert, I planted a couple of rows of two-year-old spruce, close enough together to grow into a continuous screen to deter prying eyes passing up the drive into the park beyond. The dogs ensure that we are not unduly troubled by strangers – but what the eye doesn't see, the heart doesn't covet, and a lot of pheasants from my neighbour's shoot do roost and feed in the wood. As well as acting as a natural curtain, I calculated that the dense evergreens would persuade the foolish birds to spend the night where the full moon could not advertise their plump figures in tempting silhouette.

The spruce haven't done much good either. The canopy of oak trees is thicker than it looks and their shade has stunted the growth of my young trees as it did the hedge. And rabbits added insult to injury by chewing the bark severely. When a tree has its bark ringed completely round the stem, the result is said to be even more severe than the effect of shingles meeting right round a human victim's tummy. I am happy to say that neither my family nor I have had personal experience with shingles, but I can confirm that a high proportion of my young trees withered and died as a result of the rabbits' attentions.

But although Nature is often very wasteful, she is rarely suicidal, and a small proportion of my planting has survived and will, I hope, grow into useful trees one day. It will simply take longer than I had calculated.

The damage inflicted on the trees by deer

39. PERSPECTIVE

It took an uncommitted and objective mind to get things in perspective. Young William Prestwood's father is a farmer who would have welcomed his son on the Staffordshire farm where he was born and bred, but it didn't work out that way. William was as instinctively attracted to the cause of conservation as I am myself. We both see that, among the perils which afflict wildlife in our rapidly changing world, none is greater than the rapid erosion of habitat due to the mechanical revolution in farming. But we can also see that the countryside would not be the countryside it is without the generations of farmers who carved it into shape.

So young William grasped the nettle. He declined his father's invitation to join him on the farm and decided, instead, to carve himself a niche in the sphere of conservation. In 1975, he took an Honours B.Sc. degree at Birmingham University and for the dissertation he was required to submit, he wrote a thesis entitled *The Land Use and Ecology of Goat Lodge, a Nature Reserve in the Area of Needwood Forest*.

He spent hundreds of hours here, at our reserve, got an honours degree as a result of his work, and left a detailed record, seen through one eye as an academic scientist and through the other eye as an earthy, practical naturalist.

He started off by placing Goat Lodge in the perspective of the ancient Forest of Needwood of which it was once a part. Needwood, at the time of the Norman Conquest, was a huge area of native, unmanaged natural broad-leaved forest bounded by the rivers Trent, Dove and Blythe, Bagot's Wood being towards the south-west corner, about three miles from where the Blythe now runs into Blithfield Reservoir.

The Forest of Needwood had typical oak woodland clay and marl soils, and about half a dozen gnarled and hollow ancient oaks are all that remain, though the clammy clay soil, of course, is still the same. Over the last thousand years, the whole area has been subject to continuous pressures which have completely changed the habitat. Trees were felled for both timber and fuel, and the clearings left were used for arable land and grazing. The high density of stock used to fertilise the virgin soil resulted in overgrazing, though a medieval historian recorded that the most valuable resource of Needwood was its excellent pasture. Since then, many generations of trees have been planted, destroyed and replanted. It is obvious that conventional woodland management was practised from such names as Lords Coppice and Dunstal Pool Plantation; neither name suggests woods 'harking back to the mists of time'.

As William and I wandered through the wood, we were lost in admiration for predecessors with the muscle and perseverance to dig out, by hand, main ditches which today would challenge a JCB digger to show itself cost-effective. His conclusion was, as mine is, that the intrinsic value of the Goat Lodge reserve as an example of ancient forest, virtually untouched by man, was very low because the whole area of Needwood had been changing down the centuries.

He therefore looked at Goat Lodge, in context with the whole area, and found that the local woodlands that are left, of which Goat Lodge is one, are island communities, separated by ever-growing oceans of intensively cultivated farmland and vast areas of coniferous woodland. Goat Lodge, being an ecological island, has far more scientific interest because of its potential as a refuge for creatures, being remorselessly evicted from the surrounding areas which are constantly changing, than it has for intrinsic values of ancient continuity.

Having catalogued the species that were common in the area before Bagot's Wood was felled and planted with pines, or Bagot's Wood was felled and supposedly reclaimed for agriculture, William was able to show that the habitat had altered so much that the roll-call of common parkland birds, including curlew and barn owl, had dwindled there and many of the grasses and sedges had been obliterated by chemical sprays. He then carried out an extremely detailed and sophisticated analysis of the Goat Lodge reserve, from soil structure and altitude to pH values of acidity and alkalinity, with comparative rainfall and temperatures over the whole area.

Oak and birch in Holly Covert

It was for William, of course, purely an exercise in scientific detection, relating effect to cause for the wildlife of my unimportant little wood. Unimportant, that is, to everyone but him and me! For his tutors, it was the yardstick by which his ability as a scientist to describe and analyse a microcosm of changing habitat could be measured. But for me, his thesis was much more. It was very much an independent and objective assessment of the potential of this place as a guinea pig for experiments in management of quite ordinary habitat by ordinary, amateur naturalists which, if proved successful, could be copied in other places, to the great benefit of highly pressurised wildlife.

He defined Holly Covert not as important ancient woodland but as:

1) Semi-natural oak woodland with
   a) Mature oak, with varied shrub and field layers.
   b) Mature oak with varied field layer, but poor shrub layer and regeneration.
   c) Mature oak, interspersed with pure birch stands; varied field layer.
   d) Mature oak and birch; no shrub layer and very poor field layer.

No punches pulled there and, if he had written his thesis before I started my work at Goat Lodge, I might have packed it in before going any further! But he was more cheerful about the pines (from my point of view!).

2) Coniferous plantation
   a) Pure pine stands (which are now giving most trouble).
   b) Pine dominant with regenerating oak and birch (now cleared for Lords Coppice Christmas tree patch).
   c) Birch and hazel thickets with pine present (now cleared for deer lawn).
3) Scrub.
4) Open ground: paddock, Daffodil Lawn and rides (and now deer glade).
5) Wet areas.

William made repeated visits over the seasons, cataloguing the plants scientifically by quadrat, compiling a comprehensive list of birds and mammals; I helped where I could and he received co-operation from the relevant specialists of the County Naturalist Trust for butterflies and moths.

The thesis formed an exhaustive survey of the habitat, a veritable mini-Domesday Book, which reached the firm conclusion that, from the wildlife viewpoint, the surrounding area which had once formed the ancient Forest of Needwood had deteriorated because of extensive clearing, softwood planting and intensive and chemical husbandry. Without dynamic management for the specific needs of wildlife, Goat Lodge would suffer a similar fate.

We discussed – and he included in the thesis – my plans to improve the limiting factors of food supply, to provide security and seclusion, and to control predators as a gamekeeper would. He answered the doubt that abnormally high densities of wildlife would over-exploit the available resources by pointing out that populations of animals and birds settle overcrowding by driving the surplus onto surrounding habitat. This, of course, is precisely my aim as I believe that by adequate management the decline in many species can be halted – and the surplus will

The Christmas tree patch in
Lords Coppice

move to more accessible places where the public can enjoy them without harming
them by intrusive pressure. He did not duck – or criticise – the sensitive issue
of introducing any native species, such as small-leaved limes, which can thrive
in these surroundings, although many academic purists would.

One point on which we both agree is the question of what he terms 'island
biogeography', which is jargon for saying that most wildlife needs some natural
cover to move or migrate from place to place. That is one of the main reasons
for deploring the grubbing out of hedgerows, apart from the obvious harm caused
by lack of breeding cover and food. But many animals and some birds use the
continuous cover of hedges to migrate to new territory and, if the hedges are
removed, the creatures are left on an 'island', and will not expose themselves
to unknown dangers by crossing open spaces. Because it is a predominantly dairy
farming area, much of the land consists of small, well-hedged fields, and the difficulty does not arise.

It was a stimulating association while it lasted, and after qualifying and doing
a stint with the Nature Conservancy, William Prestwood is a self-employed con-
sultant in wildlife management. The greatest compliment he paid me in his thesis
was: 'This is the first time in a thousand years of man's effective association with
Needwood Forest that he has made a conscious attempt to reconstruct a diverse,
stable ecosystem.' It gives me great encouragement.

40. WELCOME STRANGER

If it is true, as I believe, that Nature never stands still, then habitat and its inhabitants must be forever changing – for better or for worse. Our own countryside has changed more in my generation than for centuries before because of the impact of a sophisticated mechanical and chemical revolution and because the cost of labour is now prohibitive.

When I was young, farm labourers worked for twenty-eight shillings a week (just £1.40 in modern money), so it was economic to use them for digging and clearing ditches by hand, or for skilled jobs, like hedge-laying. In those more civilised days, mothers used to find the time to teach their children the names of the wildflowers; now such flowers are often classed as weeds and obliterated by chemical sprays. Hedgerow trees were spared by skilled hedge-layers because they added beauty to the landscape – and also because they might come in useful, one day, to fell and cleave for hedge stakes. Conversely, when corn was less than £20 a ton, it wasn't worth the labour of draining odd damp corners or filling in little pools by hand for the sake of a few extra bags of wheat.

Nowadays, mechanical hedgecutters, waltzing along hedgerows at six miles an hour, haven't time to stop for the odd sapling or small tree that gets in the way. It's cheaper to fell and burn it. And a JCB digger – as I know very well

Digging out Middle Pool

– is very economical for draining odd patches or filling in a little pool. All sorts of wildlife suffer as a result, but small reserves, like this, of no great economic potential, can compensate for the loss if managed not for surplus food production but for sadly pressurised wildlife instead.

So I regard my reserve not as a last stronghold for embattled wildlife but as a new colony to which endangered plants and creatures can retreat. Whatever the purists say about invalidating the records that chart disaster, I have no compunction about introducing new species which make a nonsense of these records if, by so doing, I can save a bird or beast.

The discovery of the wild service tree on Daffodil Lawn caused a local ecological sensation because, the experts said, it 'proved continuity with the ancient Forest of Needwood'. The small-leaved limes in Holly Covert came from a friend and owe descent to small-leaved limes in Sherwood Forest, the primroses and cowslips came from commercial packets of seed and the teasel in the ha-ha started life in Herefordshire.

The distinguished ecologist, Sir Dudley Stamp, proclaimed that 'the general tendency of the conservation movement is to conserve what we have and not to risk introductions'. It is perfectly true that the introduction – whether by accident or design – of brown rats, grey squirrels and mink was a disaster. But my introductions are mainly transfers of native plants or animals to habitat where there are few adverse pressures to affect their survival. To prohibit such introductions is, in my eyes, the defeatist attitude of those who forever whinge about our misfortunes but do nothing to improve them.

One of my early, purely innocent experiments could now land me in court, if not in jail. We made the small Middle Pool, on the eastern edge of Cockshutt Close, when we were putting up the deer fence. A very deep ditch, cut through the wood, crossed the boundary there and continued down to empty in Ash Brook. It was an extremely deep gully, difficult to fence, so I suggested to the contractor that, if he wished to level up the ride with his JCB, to give the fence a level bottom, that was all right by me.

He was an honest man and didn't want to take advantage of my stupidity, so he warned me that water which ran through the ditch would back up and drown half an acre or so by making it unfit for pines. I couldn't have cared less about the pines but was delighted to have a pool made for nothing – although I did get a twitch of conscience when he got his bulldozer bogged!

The joke was on me for quite a while, however, because the pool was fed by drainage water from the wood which had percolated through acid peat so that any water weed we put in turned up its toes and died. I introduced a colony of newts but there was so little cover for them that they fell easy prey to the herons. I moaned about this on a radio programme and a complete stranger, from the other side of Stafford, sent me a bag of plants I didn't recognise. They turned out to be water soldiers, and they thrived at once and have since taken over more than half the pool. They have long iris-like leaves, spread instead of standing erect, and the mass of them provide enough cover for both smooth and crested newts to breed.

Harvest mice reared in the study were liberated in the wood but sadly appear not to have survived

Water soldiers are now protected by law

I mention this shamelessly because it occurred some years before the Wildlife and Countryside Act was passed; the Act gives water soldiers, among other plants, protection so that it would be an offence to move them now without permission from On High. By coincidence, the first successful prosecution under the Act was for taking water soldiers without such absolution – and the offender was fined £200.

Above Primrose Dell, there is a nice area of thick cover including great thickets of wild rose, and I wondered if harvest mice would thrive there. They are our smallest native mouse, and I have described, in *No Badgers in My Wood*, how I bred thirty-five harvest mice in my study and turned them out in the wood. Later I swapped the breeding stock of harvest mice for some grass snakes and turned them out in the thick undergrowth round the pool at Primrose Dell.

We haven't seen the mice since, though they are so small and the cover so thick that it doesn't mean that none of them survived. My neighbour's shepherd reported seeing grass snakes (for the first time ever) in his compost heap and, the next year, two or three turned up on the edge of Dunstal Pool, so I hope with luck we have started a local colony.

I mention these two examples to explain just how difficult wildlife management is. It is easy to scoff at fishermen who get unnaturally high populations of their stew-bred trout cut down to size by herons, but I've shown that the same thing happened when I tried to introduce newts to heron territory – and weasels were the likely 'control' that decimated the harvest mice.

Judicious feeding has multiplied the flocks of finches which come to the paddock, and some stay to breed while their fellows seek alternative nesting sites. But the sparrow hawks play havoc with them so that it is easy to sympathise with gamekeepers who get a bit trigger-happy when their jobs may depend on the number of game they produce since, to hawks, poults are just as tasty as finches. I don't mind, of course, because there is great satisfaction in having the hawks nesting in the reserve when, only a few short years ago, they had almost been exterminated by eating prey that was dying from the effects of poisonous pesticides.

Since my own sporting instincts are not far below the surface, I confess without shame that I take delight in watching the clinical efficiency of wild hawks' hunting technique. Their attack has the finesse of a perfectly timed bombing run. They swoop in, over Dunstal Pool, across Middle Ride and under cover of the trees on the edge of the paddock. When they burst, at full speed, into the open, the fate of one unwary finch is almost always sealed. The art of flying trained birds in the ancient sport of falconry is poor tack by comparison.

I do not, of course, count sparrow hawks amongst my introductions. They are simply a spin-off from the policy of encouraging their prey species by management of habitat. Whether the purists would count this as a blessing or a curse, I neither know nor care. So far as my patch is concerned, it is one of my successes and, as a bonus, the damage they do to other species here grows less each season as protective habitat gradually improves and the total of small birds in the wood increases.

41. LIFE CYCLE

The odds against being struck by a thunderbolt are said to be enormous – but those, like me, living in woodland must sometimes wonder.

A group of oak trees at the bottom of the paddock, just over the border to Dunstal Pool Plantation, are uniform in size and age and their crowns are lower than the woodland either side because they grow in the hollow that fills the pool with water draining from the wood.

Thunderstorms have always held great fascination for me, and I was sitting at my study desk, idly watching forked lightning displaying the art of pyrotechnics in the sky. Counting the seconds between clap and flash indicated that the storm was over the village, about a mile away, and drifting in this direction. Then, without warning, there was an almighty clap, with simultaneous flash, in the plantation a hundred yards away. The clap was sharper than usual because it exactly coincided with the staccato crack of a great tree trunk, riven from crown to root by the irresistible force of the electric storm. It was easy to see why countryfolk

Riven by the storm, this branch will be left for insects and birds

believe that it takes a solid thunderbolt, which falls from the sky, to destroy such giant trees as this.

Why it chose that particular tree, anonymous in its group of apparently identical fellows, was impossible to guess. Theoretically, it should have struck one of those a hundred yards away, at the top of the slope, for they were higher. But it was an object lesson about the fragility of life, because any living thing, either man or beast, who had sheltered from the storm beneath that tree, would not be here to tell the tale.

When the storm was spent, I went out to examine the damage and discovered from the scorch marks that, from my ringside seat, I had witnessed a 'thunderbolt' rip through solid oak as if it were tissue. It was a visual sermon on the uncertainties of life — and perhaps on immortality as well because countryfolk say that stormstruck trees won't burn again so it is a waste of time sawing them into logs.

I don't know how true that is because I didn't try. I had been too close for comfort and had the spooky feeling that I was meant to leave Nature to bury her dead. I left the stricken carcase to rot into food for the larvae of woodboring beetles which, in turn, would be eaten by the birds, creating an endless food chain which would stretch into eternity.

We use sound branches spelched off in storms or whole birch trees which are beginning to die back for firewood because we love winter evenings by the open log fire — and have never bought fuel for the grate since we arrived. But I am a deliberately untidy woodman and leave dead trees to moulder where they fall. As they rot, they become victualled with insects, the start of an important food chain (*see* page 171). The boring tidiness of city parks does not offer half the hospitality.

But some trees are a mighty long time a-dying. In the corner of Daffodil Lawn, where it joins up to Holly Covert, there is an ancient oak with a trunk five feet across. There is no means of knowing how tall it was because the crown has long since fallen out, the bark stripped off — or most of it — and, although still iron-hard, the underlying wood is as dead as the dodo. All, that is, but one solitary surviving branch.

It must have been a very big branch in its day because it is still twenty-five feet from its tip to where it joins the trunk. It no longer points skyward because, long years before we came, it split off from the main trunk and subsided gracefully to the ground. All that attaches it to the trunk is a tiny sliver of bark — but even that is sufficient to allow enough sap to rise and flow the full length of the branch to the twigs, struggling bravely for survival at the tip. It is a vivid example of tenacity to life because the past, four or five centuries ago, is linked to the present only by that fragile little bit of bark. Each year we think will be its last — but it will probably confound such pessimism by growing fresh leaves in spring when our generation has long since returned to dust.

The ancient oak has but one surviving branch which gets its sustenance via a tiny strip of bark connecting it to the trunk

Close association with such a small patch as ours breeds an intimate knowledge which would be impossible for casual visitors. I am out in the wood at all hours and weathers, and it is always exciting to go out after a particularly heavy storm.

The first priority is to walk the boundary to check that no trees have blown down and taken the fence with them. It's panic stations when one has because it has to be cut up into manageable-sized sections with the chain-saw and lugged clear of the fence which then may have to be cobbled across the gap temporarily until it is possible to get new support posts in and make a decent repair job.

Most trees come down on the edge of rides or in recent clearings created by cutting down some pines to give space and light to broad-leaved trees which were previously fighting a losing battle for survival. Where fast-growing soft-woods are planted, they protect each other from the wind, but some unseasonal gust from a strange direction will overbalance one, as will a heavy fall of wet and sticky snow, and such unmourned casualties end up as logs for burning.

One night, there was a quite exceptional wind which did not blow a conventional gale but ripped through the wood in a single, inexplicable narrow swath. It went through Holly Covert diagonally, from the driveside a hundred yards north of the Lodge, to the junction of Daffodil Lawn and Cockshutt Close. The path it tore between the trees was not straight but gently curving and the whole force had obviously been channelled into a narrow path no more than ten feet wide.

Nobody doubts the power of water because it is easy to stand and stare at a river in flood, witnessing at first hand that little resists the path of a violent flood. Abnormal gales are even more spectacular because the havoc they wreak is there for all to see, but objects are blown away or shattered, apparently on command, because there is no visible driving force, as is the case with water.

There was no doubt about the path the storm took through our wood because, although great oaks survived, it blew down a swath of birch trees like a pack of cards. Some of them were two feet or so across the trunk, and had obviously passed their prime. Others were relatively young but were skittled over with equal lack of ceremony. When the storm was past, a blast of bombs would have left no more devastation, and I called in Fred to delete all traces of the 'morning after' with his chain-saw.

We discussed and argued about what could have set the course of the wind and I formulated an unprovable theory based on my own intimate knowledge.

One of my favourite times for seeing what shares life with me is late on summer evenings, when daylight has faded into dusk. The snag in such sorties is that, on summer evenings, the whole woodland air is literally humming with mosquitoes which can make life unbearable. Going there so often, it gradually dawned on me that some parts of the covert seemed to be infested worse than others and I charted an optimum route through the wood which happened to run diagonally from near the house across to the north-east corner of the covert, and was relatively free from hungry midges. This turned out to be the precise path along which the hurricane chose to knock down all the trees!

So perhaps the wind has favourite channels, charted as clearly as rivers and streams – but not visible to our eyes because wind is less obvious than water. If that is a viable solution for the swath of devastated trees, it would also explain summer draughts and eddies of cold air that would banish the mosquitoes.

42. LOVE/HATE

I confess to having an odd love/hate relationship with deer because however attractive they are, they do inflict quite a lot of damage to young, growing trees. Deer and newts were the creatures that first fired my love of natural history, though the newts came about twenty years before the deer because I used to catch them in the Black Country swags that were the playgrounds of my childhood.

Years later, I used to get up at crack of dawn to watch the wild deer on Cannock Chase, and struck up a lifelong friendship with Gerald Springthorpe, who knows more about wild deer than any man I know.

When the tame fallow fawn I had at our previous house went to Frances Pitt, the naturalist (*see* page 62), I was given a foundling roe deer kid which I bottle-reared and which grew up to be one of the tamest and most delightful animals that I have ever met. She came here with us and settled happily but, although I got a wild buck and doe to go with her, she never bred nor even mated in the ten years that she lived.

When she died I reared Honey, a white fallow doe, who came as a gift from a friend who owns an ancient deer park. She acts as a decoy by persuading the wild deer in the wood that we are harbingers of sanctuary not doom, and that where she finds it safe to go is also safe for them, and she is still around, thirteen

My foundling roe deer shares the goose's corn

long years later. She has produced eleven fawns and reared ten, she is breathtakingly beautiful, and is confident enough to come boldly up, not only to eat out of my hand but out of the hand of any guest who brings her goodies. Small wonder, then, that I fell hopelessly and irrevocably in love with her and that I put welcome on the mat for all her fellows.

The herd thrived and multiplied and, at first, there was plenty for them to eat because birch scrub grew thick where the softwood trees are planted. Deer do not graze so much as browse, being fond of the broad leaves of bramble and hawthorn, oak and bilberry, birch and other broad-leaved plants, trees and bushes. The more birch they ate, the less my conscience pricked about not weeding the pines.

But nothing stands still in Nature and the surviving birch grew on upwards and their attraction seemed to be in inverse ratio to their height. The fickle deer transferred their attentions to the young oaks and bilberry – which were just showing the first signs of recovery from predation by the goats. There were good bramble breaks in Cockshutt Close and Ley Close, also recovering from the goats, but the deer pruned them back and with every patch of cover they took, they wore a bit more off their welcome. It was partly the goats' fault, of course, because the damage goats can do has to be seen to be believed. But the contributory factor was that the deer were thriving so well that their numbers escalated.

Gerald, ever practical, suggested that we must cull some. A rough rule of thumb is that it is necessary to remove annually about one deer in six to maintain the herd at a static size. More taken out and the herd will shrink. With fewer removed, the numbers will escalate.

When the Forestry Commission surrendered the lease, they went away and left everything as it was, including an observation tower which they had erected so deer wardens could sit and wait, with a rifle, to shoot selected deer from above without unforeseen dangers from ricocheting bullets. The deer had recovered from the severe stress caused when we had a heavy cull to avoid my new neighbour suffering damage to his crops (*see* page 65), so Gerald climbed into the old high seat to do a selective cull of those within our perimeter fence.

No British wild animal has a greater colour range than fallow deer which literally vary from white to black. Honey, my hand-reared deer, was ginger when she arrived as a fawn. As she grew and developed, her coat lightened until it was white, though she has normal-coloured eyes instead of pink, so is not a true albino. Between the less usual black and white is a common colour form that is dark dun in winter but moults out to a lovely reddish fawn in summer, often with a few white spots.

Prettiest of all, perhaps, the Bambis of fiction are technically called menil. This is a lovely spotted fawn, like the summer coats of deer that are dark dun in winter. But menil spots are whiter and their golden russet coats are brighter. When Gerald culled selectively, he left a fair proportion of menil, but we tried to keep at least one example of each colour in the herd.

The snag was that Gerald *hates* killing deer more than any job he does because

ed Honey, my white
w doe, on the bottle
een years ago – she still
s as good as new and
uced another fawn this

he regards them with far more affection than any theoretical combination of wild-flowers and vegetation. He found every reason for never culling quite as many as we had agreed and therefore the size of the herd gradually increased – and my coveted understorey grew less instead of more.

A perfectly genuine reason for his failing to hit the numbers target was that the herd divided fairly spontaneously into two separate social groups. Honey was the dominant doe in one group which she brought to graze close to the windows of the Lodge, all of which were tame enough to feed at the bird-table, a sight which always delights our friends as much as us. They happened to include a fairly wide colour range so that the obvious thing was to take most of the planned annual cull from the other group which were not so tame and would be missed less, for the simple reason that we did not see them so often anyway.

When Gerald climbed into his high seat and waited for the group we wanted to come out into the open, he took one shot all right – and got one deer – but the rest of the group then bunched up with Honey's lot and it was thenceforth impossible to know which belonged to which and the operation had to be aborted because the whole herd naturally became so spooky. As a result, we always failed to cull the numbers we planned, the herd increased in size and the coveted cover declined.

Gerald and I worked out a plan which is more effective. In the winter, we

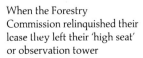

When the Forestry Commission relinquished their lease they left their 'high seat' or observation tower

feed the deer onto Daffodil Lawn which is surrounded with high netting. At the same time, we also bait the paddock in front of the house with a little grain. As a result, the two social groups feed at the same time but at opposite ends of the wood.

Next to the entrance (or exit!) gate on the lawn, we have constructed a long, narrow 'crush', like a conventional cattle crush, finishing in a narrow, boarded catch-up pen, fitted with a series of sliding doors. When the tame doe and her retinue are feeding near the house, I sneak down the other end and shut the gate onto Daffodil Lawn. Next morning, I inspect what is feeding there and, if they are not the ones we want to cull, I open the gate and let them walk out. If they are the ones we want, I open the gate to the crush, which is next to the exit, a helper appears from behind, and they stream into the crush, in mistake for what they think is the gate back to the wood. Any we do not want to keep we can let back to the wood, one by one, and cull the rest quietly and humanely, without alarming the survivors.

Some of the venison from those we cull goes into our deep freeze, we give a joint to our close friends and sell some to game dealers, putting the proceeds into the fencing-fund. From time to time we sell a few 'on the hoof', alive, to provide fresh blood to herds in private deer parks, but this outlet has to be strictly limited to friends we can trust as there is a danger that unscrupulous dealers would promise 'good homes' but export abroad where the animals' plight could be so unpleasant that humane slaughter would be far kinder. Any form of deer 'control' is an unpleasant job, but it is absolutely vital to restrict the size of the herd to prevent them literally eating themselves out of house and home.

I have had great pleasure from the muntjac deer which are non-native 'introductions' by any standards and are rather frowned on by the Forestry Commission who object to them fraying young trees. They were introduced about the turn of the century by the same Duke of Bedford who also introduced grey squirrels. Escapees from the ducal park at Woburn, mainly after the last war, have been colonising the country, occurring about twenty miles further from Woburn each year. This is because they love dense cover, but are natural wanderers and therefore find crops of standing corn or hay ideal sanctuary. They are only about the size of a fox – indeed, they are very foxy coloured and could easily be mistaken for one as they creep through thickets.

I was given a buck and doe kid, at an interval of twelve months, and I reared both on the bottle so that they grew up as tame as robins. They came and went freely through my study window, being naturally 'house-trained' because muntjac defecate at chosen latrine sites, partly to delineate their territory. They were completely fearless with the dogs.

As they matured, they became gradually more and more independent until they ceased to come in the house, and instead lived and bred in the wood, mixing with wild muntjac which had also colonised it. Visitors seeing them in their summer russet pelage often mistake them for foxes but, though they are frequently referred to as barking deer, we only hear their harsh, rasping voice (which indeed could be mistaken for that of a fox) at very infrequent intervals.

43. FIRE AND WATER

Men of all ages, from nine to ninety, love playing with fire and water.

Primrose Dell is one of my favourite habitats in the whole wood. When we came, it was a bare marl pit, stripped of the decency of all trees by the chap who bought the timber and Fred with his efficient lop-and-top. It was possible to stand on the southern lip of the basin and look downhill to the ditch dividing the park from us, with nothing to obstruct the view.

As I described on page 43, the Forestry Commission had added insult to injury by their repeated efforts to plant the dell with their beastly little pines – and I had added injury to insult by vandalising them until attempts to plant it fizzled out, rescuing the primroses from certain oblivion. The dell has been one of my pets ever since because it is living proof of winning the first – and last – battle in an undeclared war. It established relative strengths and, thereafter, we got on fine with the Forestry without having to call each other's bluff again.

Now I can stand on the same vantage point and see no more than twenty yards because thickets of hawthorn, wild rose and blackthorn have filled the space where pines were planned to grow. Badgers live and breed in the artificial sett we made and the ditch I cut to keep their kennel dry is crossed by a plank bridge which, by being coated with an inch of muddy silt, discloses nightly traffic by badger footprints being left in the mud.

Water-crowsfoot on Primrose Dell

A 'controlled' burn of the bracken patch where I hope the gorse will bloom

The pool in the basin bottom was originally a puny pit, eight yards or so across, which had filled with water when the marl had been excavated to fertilise the land. We had enlarged it when we put in the deer fence but, as with Middle and Dunstal Pools, the water from the acid peat would not support plant life so that frogs, newts and toads which ventured to try to breed there did not have sufficient cover and were snapped up by the herons.

What was desperately needed was dense vegetation to support not only food for newts but the wide variety of insect life which would be attractive to waterfowl.

Gerald and I scrumped whole trailer-loads of waterweed from far and wide, and at last hit the jackpot with water mint and water crowsfoot which we took from a similar local marl pit. Besides wild daffodils and primroses on the banks, the surface of the water grew white with the crowsfoot and, when I'd given a pair of prospective resident coot the fright of their lives for being so aggressive to all competitors with feathers, they went away and were replaced by a pair of breeding dabchicks which, to my eyes, are among the most attractive of our native waterfowl.

Nothing in Nature is certain and, long before we had decided to rest on our laurels, the water level started to fall, with no sign of any leak. Checking with everyone I knew, I discovered that the Story Brook, a powerful stream through the middle of Bagot's Park, was also drying up for no apparent reason. Everybody's water level, it seemed, was sinking out of sight. The Regional Officer of the Nature Conservancy called socially but not officially and, on a stroll round the wood, I was interested to hear his caustic comment that this was once an interesting pool. 'Was once' indeed!

About thirty yards away, my boundary with the park is delineated by a deep ditch which takes off all the drainage from more than a hundred acres of Squitch Bank, the southern edge of the old deer park. Before the park was reclaimed for agriculture, water trickled down this ditch, seven days a week, fifty-two weeks a year. Modern efficient drainage, with a drain about every twenty-two yards, now meant that after heavy rain, an almost immediate surge of water slurped down the ditch which was soon dry again. There was no time for the water to soak into the thirsty soil to be conserved and continuously released slowly enough to keep the water in Primrose Dell topped up.

I decided, therefore, to spend the cash from my first little stand of Christmas trees on connecting this ditch to the pool. I was quoted £180 to cut a trench with a JCB, lay a large-diameter drainage pipe in the bottom and backfill with the soil dug from the trench. This had to be over seven feet deep at its deepest, but when it was done, there was a steep fall so that the surge of water after rain would scour away any silt that had settled in the pipe.

In dry times, nothing flows at all, but when there is a fall of rain, every drop falling over the hundred acres sluices down the ditch and through my pipe to top up the level in the pool in Primrose Dell. The surplus flows through the normal outlet that was there before. I put paving stones in the bottom of the ditch to stop the water eroding the dam, so that, when we get a downpour, the level rises and only a little passes through my pipe, while the surplus flows on along the ditch and does not bung up my pool with silt.

It all works like a dream because even an odd few hours of rain are all that is needed to keep the pool filled to the brim.

The main worry for the future is the quality of the water. Before we interfered to prevent the old pool drying out, what did find its way from the wood was clear and pure rain which only had had to percolate through the acid peat. Now, there is abundant water to keep the pool topped up, but it has been collected from drainage off intensively fertilised plough. There may be surplus nitrates and other salts so powerful that the crowsfoot may be choked and replaced by flannelweed and other undesirable vegetation which is encouraged by those who let artificial fertilisers leech into watercourses. The first result, in winter, has been turgid water, as thick as potato soup. With luck, it will clear by spring, and perhaps broad-leaved pondweed may grow lush enough to shade out the flannelweed.

I was between the devil and his mate because it was really the choice between the pool drying up to a puddle that would support nothing, or taking the risk of getting a full pool, relatively unaffected by temporary drought, but with water that might may be polluted by intensive husbandry. We have taken the risk as the lesser of the evils.

Bracken has been another major curse because it is so invasive and, when it thrives, it shades out virtually everything rash enough to try to survive beneath its canopy. There is one patch of about an acre between the pines of Cockshutt Close and Ley Close and the ride along the edge of Holly Covert and Daffodil Lawn. As I've described on page 128, I tried to kill this bracken by paddocking enough pigs to mutilate and uproot it to extinction, but it wasn't a very successful experiment, and the bracken continued to flourish.

So I decided to convert the area to a gorse cover which long-tailed tits and other small birds would relish as ideal nesting cover. It would be grand cover for hares and muntjac deer, woodcock and butterflies, and the only snag would be that gorse is so invasive that it might not submit to being constrained by boundaries I selected. The pines on two sides were dense enough to allow nothing to thrive in their acidic needles or in the lethal shade of their interwoven branches. I mow the rides on the open sides with the tractor and jungle-busting chain-swipe which would pulverise any seedlings which strayed from the chosen patch.

I flattened a firebreak, between bracken and wood, with tractor and roller, and Fred duly turned up to burn the bracken. It is a highly skilled job along a woodland edge – too exciting for comfort if you own the wood! But my confidence in Fred is limitless so I put on half the gorse seed before he burned the patch, to scorch the seed. When he was done, I disc-harrowed the burnt bracken and sowed the soil with the rest of the seed.

Time will tell if the ploy has worked but if not, and the bracken returns, I shall spray it with Asulox and kill it once and for all, because I am determined to have my gorse cover to give yet more exciting variety of habitat. I hate poisonous herbicides and pesticides, but bracken is unappetising as a food for wildlife so that the risk is minimal, especially as Asulox is not persistent and is soon rendered safe by time and rain. We may 'plant pears for our heirs', but gorse should give quicker results, and be infinitely more attractive than bracken.

...takes great care to keep
...re under control and away
...the trees

44. AMENITIES PROVIDED

The least skilled gamekeeper has no difficulty in rearing pheasants because he uses precisely the same methods as any intensive poultry breeder. An electric incubator hatches the eggs at anything up to a thousand at a time, and he rears the chicks under a thermostatically-controlled brooder, heated by electricity or bottle gas and maintained at a predetermined temperature. He prevents the diseases of intensive husbandry by feeding the chicks on preconstituted food pellets, laced with enough antibiotics to annihilate the most virulent bugs.

What separates the men from the boys is the ability to persuade the growing poults, once they have been turned loose in the wood, to stick around until the shooting season starts. For this, the skilled gamekeepers of my youth relied on their own stockmanship and ability as naturalists instead of the sales gimmicks of the agrochemical industry. They also encouraged the wild pheasants to breed by controlling their predators but collected clutches of eggs laid in vulnerable spots and hatched them under domestic broody hens.

Managing wildlife demands precisely the same skills. The first essential is to provide attractive breeding habitat to persuade the desired species to settle willingly and, when the adults have bred, there must be enough suitable food, supplied naturally or artificially, to rear the young which, with luck, will adopt the territory of their birth to breed in future seasons.

Most people who enjoy watching birds at close quarters put food out for them in the winter. Bird-tables groan under the weight of fat and household scraps, cheese rind and rotten apples. Those who have got the message that such hospitality pays are rewarded by flocks of tom tits and starlings, blackbirds and robins and a sprinkling of much-vaunted rarer species.

Our local butcher is one of the dying breed of skilled men who still have a licence to slaughter on the premises. He sells truly delicious meat because he chooses beasts which are neither too lean for flavour nor stuffed with hormones and antibiotics, because he deals with farmers who have not been seduced into factory farming which produces quantity at the expense of quality.

He puts aside great hunks of rough suet for my birds and the belly fat from luscious tripes; these I melt in an ex-army cook pot, on a bottle gas-ring in the tractor shed because the aromas of my cuisine are not to everybody's taste. The local tits, nuthatches and pied woodpeckers therefore feed on fat fit for avian gourmets when they accept my invitation to dine outside our windows.

I offer monkey nuts and flaked maize, in wire mesh baskets, for dessert and Jess scrounges fruit that is past its saleable prime for the thrush and blackbird tribe. We scatter wheat in the paddock for the pheasants and finches — and the deer have no scruples about joining them at dinner. The guests we attract range from game birds to scores of smaller species which hang around all winter in far higher concentrations than where subsidiary food is absent so that, when winter brightens into spring, we start off with a healthy population of prospective breeding birds.

Robins occupy quiet woodland as readily as town gardens

Seclusion suits the herons and many of the shy small birds but a number of the woodland birds need holes and crevices in dead or dying trees. In an 'untidy' wood like ours, trees past their prime are left to die in peace and rot back until they return to the earth where they sprouted from seeds, decades or even centuries ago. This is a deliberate policy because rotting wood supports a wealth of beetles and wood-boring insects which, in turn, supply ideal natural food for woodpeckers and other birds. They also supply nesting holes, where branches have broken or other breaches made, causing the internal wood to soften or rot.

Although I trap and shoot them, grey squirrels take some of the birds and, if birds nest in a hole with an entrance large enough to admit a squirrel, there is a real danger that the eggs will be robbed or chicks killed and eaten. Therefore, I erect a number of specially constructed nest boxes. They would be very expensive to buy but the Royal Society for the Protection of Birds, of The Lodge, Sandy, Bedfordshire, issue an excellent, practical booklet on the subject. This lists and illustrates a number of artificial nesting containers, ranging from plastic or

uthatches are back and ng on the bird fat we de

concrete 'saucers' for house martins, to wooden boxes for hole-nesting birds ranging from tits to owls and kestrels. They are not only clearly described and illustrated, but all the dimensions are noted, including the best diameter for entrance holes, to suit the desired species whilst excluding others which might disturb or prey on them.

They are as suitable for suburban gardens as they are for my wood, and the kestrel nesting platform was once so successful that it persuaded a pair of city-slicker kestrels that a high-rise block of flats was really a cliff face, and they nested in an artificial nesting box on a thirteenth-storey window sill!

I have had nothing so spectacular but I have made a whole variety of boxes which have been tenanted, over the years, by tits and nuthatches, kestrels and flycatchers, wagtails and robins and tree creepers, all of which have more than paid their rent by the pleasure they have given.

The complement to such work is the provision of suitable, natural habitat,

Barn owls are sadly becoming very rare

from bramble brakes to gorse thickets, the island on the pool (where the Canada geese rear our Christmas dinner – *see* page 199), and the open scrub among the Christmas trees in Lords Coppice where we still hope the nightjars and grasshopper warblers will return.

If you are thinking of following suit, do not be limited by birds. On page 200, I have described the 'drain', or artificial earth, provided by generations of sportsmen for foxes, and I am sure it would work as well in many a suburban garden as it does in our wood – and foxes, feeding on the patio, would be a novel treat for dinner guests! Our badger setts have been equally successful – and the signs are that, like foxes, badgers are growing more urbanised than anyone would have thought possible a generation ago, when I started working with them, so I hope that others will supply amenities for badgers as well.

But perhaps the most worthwhile guests to attract are bats because they are in more danger than almost any other species. The dreaded scientists have been at it again, this time providing an obscene insecticide to kill deathwatch beetles and woodworm in the roofs of houses. Not only have they spelt death to the beetles, they have also exterminated thousands of bats which formerly shared the roofspace. The plight of bats grew so grave that special protection has had to be provided, under the Wildlife and Countryside Act, and it is now illegal even to disturb them, far less kill them.

I persuaded a colony of pipistrelle bats to settle in my roofspace, long before it was necessary to protect them. My motive was far more simple for I get endless pleasure watching their acrobatics as they hawk flying insects in the gloaming. I was delighted, therefore, when the colony of little flittermice was joined by a smaller colony of more spectacular long-eared bats, which still share our roofspace.

Now that the peril is more widespread, Bob Stebbings, a practical naturalist attached to the scientific wing of the Nature Conservancy, has compiled a booklet giving designs and dimensions of roosting boxes for bats, similar to the RSPB booklet on nest boxes for birds. Gerald Springthorpe has been working with bat specialists for years, by erecting scores of bat boxes on Commission land, with the result that the bat population has increased enormously, greatly benefiting the trees because the bats eat so may insect pests.

My only criticism of such joint ventures is that the scientists always seem to want to disturb the creatures by catching them and fitting them with numbered metal rings, as they do with birds. What reward they get in exchange for the stress of capture and the inconvenience and pain caused by clipping metal rings onto the wings of bats is quite beyond my comprehension.

I have made exact copies of the bat boxes used by the Commission, to the NCC design, and Gerald has helped with advice about the best sites to erect them in the wood. Some of them have been occupied and, if my craftsmanship is not quite up to the professional standard, at least the tenants are never ringed or disturbed by meddling specialists in bat behaviour. They may think it rather churlish of me to deny them access to my guests, but I trust the birds and bats have no complaints.

45. VISITATION

In 1982 a youth arrived from the Nature Conservancy to give the place the once-over. He hardly looked the part because I mistook him for a Work Experience lad, paid for out of taxes to ease the queue for proper jobs. It appeared that his mission was to reassess the importance of individual Sites of Special Scientific Interest so that their owners could be notified whether their status would be rescheduled as protected sites or struck off into oblivion.

Those redesignated would have management agreements by which the NCC must be notified before any change of management and, if they disagreed with an intended change which might bring profit to the owner, compensation would be paid for the loss of profit their veto entailed. The media gave considerable publicity to a farmer on the Isle of Islay who is said to get £16,000 a year for *not* shooting the wild geese who eat the grass on his land because, it is alleged, he might get that much extra profit if he preserved the pasture for his sheep. Some landowners are said to have bought marginal wetland cheap and been awarded large sums on the NCC's refusal of permission to drain it, though their intention to do so was no more than a ploy to get a handout.

I wished neither for a government handout nor to be hamstrung by red tape, so I did not greet my visitor with open arms.

He was a nice enough lad, hog-tied by his tight terms of reference, but I

Pheasants will, one day, benefit from the cover provided by the rhododendrons

ant marestail grows at
mrose Dell, where there are
o the rare sedges

gathered that his worthy purpose was to recommend retention of the part of my domain which pure scientists would find interesting but to forestall claim for loss of profit on the rest by the exclusion of the less 'important' parts from the official schedule. His boss, the Regional Officer, subsequently assured me that I must have misunderstood him because he had no responsibility for what was or was not included for protection. His job was simply to do a survey of the vegetation on which bigger wheels than he would make their judgement.

Whatever the outcome, the fact remains that the success or failure of any joint management pivots on goodwill so that if the NCC sullies its public image, whether by inexperience or incompetence, they are on a hiding to nothing with their enterprise.

When we went round the wood, I was not surprised that the young adjudicator took a bit of umbrage at the rhododendrons I had planted in Holly Covert. He was not to know that the originals had been supplied by a kind colleague in his own department, and had been planted in order to make good pheasant cover from which to argue from strength with bob-the-killer keepers (*see* page 127). That was certainly too unorthodox to be included in his schedule of scientific interests.

It was puzzling that he didn't appear to notice the ancient hedge maple, the wild service tree on Daffodil Lawn or the jungle of giant marestail, all of which are emblems of antiquity. The only thing to spark light into his eyes were some sedges on the edge of the pool in Primrose Dell. Apparently, he was some sort of authority on sedges which dramatically turned him on to spout a catalogue of Latin names as if they were his litany.

We parted with no mutual regret and I phoned his boss complaining about a visitation from one on such a different wavelength. His boss, quite rightly, jumped to the lad's defence and reiterated that, in any case, his survey was circumscribed so tightly that his personal views could have no influence either way.

Nevertheless, I was acutely anxious because the management of an experimental wildlife sanctuary demands long-term plans that depend on continuity on one hand, but the freedom to make snap decisions when they are necessary. I had previously got on fine with visitors from the Nature Conservancy and respected their advice, which had been minimal, but the inexperienced surveyor had inadvertently made a chink in the curtains through which I could see the faces of lurking Big Brothers!

That survey took place in 1982 and, almost four years later, in the early spring of 1986, there had still been no official action. Even by NCC standards, this was hardly rapid progress and countless letters and phone calls only elicited the excuses of 'too busy', 'understaffed' and 'overworked' and that 'no SSSIs have been renotified in Staffordshire yet'. To substantiate his claim of overwork, the local Regional Officer, who has a wry sense of humour, started to dictate his letters but had them signed, in his absence, by a faceless bureaucrat who can afford an even droller smile because of her anonymity. She once pee-peed her boss's letter in his absence, and referred to the Infestation Control Branch of the Ministry of Agriculture as the Interpretation Control Branch! In my experience, Misinterpretation Control Branch would be both funnier and far more accurate!

The whole discussion has been conducted with good-natured jocularity but the fact remains that our basic difference is in the definition of what is or is not both scientifically interesting and important. I have maintained throughout that wildlife, including plants, insects, birds and other mammals, is under unparalleled pressure because of a mechanical revolution which makes it possible to change the landscape overnight, and the chemical technology of farming which too often results in death by poison of friends as well as foes. So I believe we should take advantage of every unused patch of land and innovate and develop management techniques to help species survive, whether they are rare or common.

At the beginning of 1984, I received a letter, giving the 'informal' opinion (without prejudice!) that the present SSSI should stay. It said that Daffodil Lawn, the heronry and oakwood (both in Holly Covert) qualified in terms of standard criteria, 'since all SSSIs must be truly outstanding, either as examples of semi-natural plant/animal associations' (whatever semi-natural means!) 'or because they support especially important populations of particular species, rare or common'.

It went on to say: 'The remainder [of the wood] is more difficult because the SSSI system is more geared to the safeguarding of existing features than to the creation of new ones by positive management.' Fifteen-all, I think, because, by any standards, the heronry is important since it contains more than 1% of the national total of nests. On the other hand, it has certainly been very carefully managed to encourage the increase from fourteen to eighty nests so is scarcely

Our herons appealed to computer minds because they had increased to more than 1% of the national population

'semi-natural'. Evidence of ridge-and-furrow ploughing in the oakwood and on Daffodil Lawn indicates that both oaks and daffs were planted so the same applies to them. There are arguments on both sides, so take your pick.

Bluebell woods are growing scarce everywhere but the high ground of Cockshutt Close is a solid blue haze around the feast of Whitsuntide. They grow so closely together that nothing survives among them but bracken, but the bluebells have flowered their fill before the bracken is mature enough to cause them any damage (*see* page 48). The bluebells are certainly 'natural' because neither I nor anyone else has lifted a finger to help them. When we clear a patch of pines, beneath which nothing has been able to flower for a decade or more, masses of foxgloves grow the following spring for the simple reason that seeds of the previous crop can lie dormant for many years to delight the world by their resurrection the first time conditions change for the better. The men from the Nature Conservancy have never, to the best of my knowledge, let the word 'bluebell' pass their lips, yet I should have thought that the bluebells and the primroses, cowslips, wild violets and marsh marigolds of Primrose Dell are as much 'semi-natural features' to be safeguarded as the wild daffs or herons' nests. None of them has been introduced, but all of them are managed.

The futility of making spot checks, to see what flora and fauna flourish, is obvious with a moment's reflection. On the untouched ground where the wild service trees grow, there are spectacular drifts of wood anemones, or windflowers, as countryfolk call them. In the dry summer of 1976, they were nearly all obliterated and botanists doing a census the following year would have marked them very scarce. But, although nothing stands still because of perpetual change, there is a miraculous tenacity to life and the windflowers have gradually recovered until they fill my eyes with pleasure once more.

So, gradually, as the foreign softwoods are consigned to oblivion, our native English wildflowers and trees will reappear and, with them, the birds and beasts who can take advantage of the return of their natural habitat.

46. FRAGRANT HARVEST

The official policy of the Ministry of Agriculture has been, for many years, Production At Any Price. Hedges have been bulldozed out to make bigger fields to build corn mountains ever higher. Ancient water meadows have been drained to make the milk lake deeper at the expense not just of higher taxes to fund such extravagance, but of the rich variety of wildflowers that took centuries to establish. Poisonous pesticides, fungicides and herbicides have increased the turgid butter-bog at the expense of butterflies.

Such nonsense had to end when it eventually dawned on politicians that the mechanical revolution combined with modern science could now produce more than we could eat. No one has yet beaten the laws of supply and demand so that either production must be cut to meet demand – or the Big Boys who can produce the cheapest food will win while the rest go to the wall. Farmers on marginal land, such as upland country or with difficult soil, will go up the spout to leave the capital-intensive corn and milk barons as survivors.

Unfortunately, much of Britain's marginal land is the most beautiful and rich in wildlife so that promoting Big Business at the expense of the Little Men could be an environmental disaster.

William Waldegrave, present Minister of State for the Environment, is a dynamic youngster aiming for high places. This was evident when he spearheaded a movement to de-vandalise the Ministry of Agriculture which forced Michael Jopling, the Minister, not so much to do a U-turn as a double somersault. Although Jopling's department had spent years recommending persistent and unselective poisonous sprays, subsidising hedge removal and the draining of ancient wetlands, the Minister suddenly sprayed himself whiter than white by announcing that he had conservation at heart!

It is of no great importance whether he and his like climb down to get the credit or if they are pushed. The prospect is that, one way or another, it is certain that huge areas of land will have to be taken out of production of their present crops and put to other uses. The increased leisure which stems from automation will give increased opportunities for more and more people to spill into the countryside, nostalgic for the pleasures of simpler things. They will want to see the wildlife and wildflowers, annihilated by the policy of Production At Any Price, restored as near as possible to their former glories. That is easier said than done – as I know to my cost!

Half way up my New Ride, on the edge of Holly Covert, is the old Forestry Commission high seat, designed for culling deer, but used by me as an observation tower which gives a view along five open woodland rides. It is virtually surrounded by woodland and there was about half an acre, just below it, where the pines had not grown because they had been overrun by bracken. It was a lovely patch where the stumps left when the previous crop of oaks were felled had rotted away, so I gave it a thorough thrashing with the chain-swipe that killed the bracken which hates mechanical disturbance.

(OPPOSITE) A sight I hope to emulate! Wildflowers grown from seeds harvested from ancient meadows

Thistles are beloved by bees and seven-coloured linnets

Thistles and nettles sprang up where bracken was before, and this suited my plans because, being surrounded by pines with an understorey of pine needles where nothing could survive, there was no danger of my nettles or thistles seeding over my boundary to annoy my neighbours. That weedy half-acre is a paradise for butterflies in summer, and for gaudy goldfinches, which we call seven-coloured linnets, when the thistles seed. I can climb into my observation tower at almost any time of the year in the certainty of seeing interesting birds or insects on the patch I created or, to be more precise, which was bequeathed to me by Nature.

I have had less luck with more exotic wildflowers because, although it is now possible to purchase seed commercially, one has to experiment to see what seeds thrive best. Most flowers need a seedbed of bare soil, teased to a hospitable tilth, but ranker 'weeds' like invasive grass, nettles or bracken cash in first and stifle the coveted wildflowers at birth, almost as effectively as the pigs clear patches of Holly Covert.

Hunters of Chester were among the first to crack the problem. They already specialise in a wide variety of grasses and they have perfected a machine, to follow a tractor, which drills in the grass seed without further cultivation, just as a farmer drills in his rows of corn. This very specialised drill is being adapted to sow wildflowers in great variety. The seed is put into the drill which inserts it below the turf and, provided the sward is kept mown short, or cropped short by grazing, the seedlings can percolate through and develop into wildflowers.

There are, of course, myriad potential snags, as is always the case with anything new. Some soils suit one species and some another, and more often than not it is only possible to discover which will thrive more by trial and error than by theories spawned in scientific labs. John Hunter advised me to take mixed seeds of, perhaps, fifty different varieties, sow some in spring and some in autumn – and wait to see what comes up! Although a soil analysis gives some pointers, variations often occur from yard to yard, as on the edges of our wood. One patch may be acid peat, built up over generations, the next a fine tilth of fertile topsoil, caused by rooting pigs or mechanical disturbance, and the next cold clammy clay, as inhospitable as an arid desert. One is only able to profit by experience.

The advantage of the specialised drill is that so many more seeds will germinate. Nature is quite incredibly wasteful. If more than a pair or so of tadpoles survived from every bucketful of frogspawn, a plague of frogs would engulf the countryside. So infertility, predation, accident and disease are sent by providence to cut them down to size. Every giant oak tree has hundredweights of acorns, but if they all germinated and prospered, there would be dense patches growing all over the place.

Wildflower seeds, scattered haphazardly on green turf, will germinate but the first spell of dry weather will kill them before their roots can struggle down to generative soil. A specialised mechanical seed-drill puts the seeds where they need to go instead of relying on chance, with astronomical odds against success. Where thirty kilos of broadcast seed may be needed for an acre, a meagre three kilos would produce better results when mechanically drilled in.

The drill developed by John Hunter to sow wildflower seeds for re-sale or amenity

Very careful management is needed afterwards. The seedlings of many wild-flowers are so delicate that, even when they have beaten heavy odds by germinating and starting growth, they will still succumb to any hostile competition. To avoid this, it is vital to keep the grass short as a lawn for the first few weeks, either by mechanical mowing or grazing.

I decided, therefore, to start with a swath of seeds along the edges of my woodland rides and round the perimeter of the deer lawn. It is an expensive experiment at around £40 a kilo – or £160 an acre – for fairly common mixed seeds, and such experiments surely justify the policy of growing cash crops such as Christmas trees to generate the money to cover possible failure. John Hunter is providing the specialised seed-drill his company has developed as well as his expert advice.

By being careful with the pennies, and sowing small areas in selected spots, I should be able, in 1987, to monitor my initial success – and it will not be catastrophic if I fail. My prediction is that such cultivations will be a major crop for future farming and this could be a lifeline for some of those hit hardest when the Ministry of Agriculture regains its sanity and stops subsidising surplus mountains. The farmers will first have to adjust to the fact that all wildflowers are not weeds. I have heard of one farmer who has multiplied his income from corn by making £1,000 per annum an acre from 'weed' seeds – which now retail as 'wildflowers'.

Even more traumatic will be the mental contortions of the Ministry bumblecrats who will have to adjust to the fact that many of the 'weeds' for which they prescribed their lethal sprays have suddenly blossomed as profitable crops. Other U-turns are not unknown, and if a few scientists have to be made redundant, the colourful countryside that will have been created will be cheap at the price.

47. OFF WITH THEIR HEADS!

One of the results of the Forestry Commission's co-operation in doing all in their power to avoid interference with what they must have regarded as my eccentric management of wildlife was that they did not get their normal high harvest from the seedling trees in my wood. The result of holding their hand was that their crop was spasmodic, thick in some areas and mighty thin in others.

The softwoods therefore developed in patches which suited me because there was more chance for a wide spectrum of wildlife in the softwood patches that had failed than there was in pine thickets that shaded out all understorey. In fact, the softwoods were not a complete environmental disaster. As I walked through the sparse patches of pines, it became obvious that quite a large number of indigenous broad-leaved trees had survived Fred's lop-and-top operation although most of them were weak and weedy specimens. In other cases, seedlings had been drawn to the light by the thickets around them or had coppiced from the stumps of the recently felled hardwoods. Whatever the cause, the fact was that the forty acres which had been leased to the Commission was not the sterile monoculture that I had feared.

On our daily walks round the wood, Jess and I discussed the programme for my future projects. We began to identify the best specimens of surviving hard-woods and I blazed the trunks of the pines around them so that the white scars where I had slashed bark from trunks identified them for slaughter the following Christmastide.

The first pines that we thus condemned were mostly close to the edges of the rides and as a result, the edge of several rides was eaten back five or ten yards into the wood, leaving any thriving broad-leaved trees with enough space around to allow growth into their natural shape. Looking along these rides in summer gradually gave the impression of an avenue of English oaks which had dominated the sombre foreign trees until they had put them in their menial place.

The next stage was for Jess and me to push through the brittle lower branches of the remaining pines in search of something more attractive. There were many self-set birch and, when we located a good specimen with a trunk six or more inches in diameter, we marked the surrounding pines to be harvested at the bottom end of the next November. We found a few nice beech and a number of hornbeam, which does well in our soil, and in wetter patches a lot of alder, though most of that was coppicing from stools left when the best timber in the wood had been felled before we arrived. No conservationist would mind because butterfly and moth caterpillars like coppiced trees as much as stately standards.

It was a dicey calculation to decide how much to take out in any one season because, strictly speaking, I suppose we should have applied for a licence but, by then, I was fed up with bureaucratic bumph and my committee-of-one decided to cut the fruitless cackle and to get on with the job before what broad-leaved trees were left were fatally swamped by the thickening pines.

Trees were felled along the woodland edge to give more light and air, and to give space for undergrowth to develop

The results are most encouraging. We made one clearing round a spindly beech five or six years ago, leaving about twice as much space around it as the midday sun on a majestic beech would cover. To our great delight the weakling tree puffed out his chest and expanded as weightlifters do when about to show the world what they are made of. In the few short years since we gave it light and air – and felled the close-packed pines which had guzzled up its water – that beech has become a specimen which fills our eyes with pleasure every time we pass it on the ride.

We naturally repeated the experiment all over the wood and it is not necessary to make a clearing more than twenty yards or so across before the space greens over with vegetation. Areas of the wood which must once have been clothed in ferns are suddenly verdant with ferns again, and the beautiful foxgloves seem to spring up from nowhere. Where the woodland lop-and-top has been consumed by bonfires, the first plant life to colonise the scorched patch are the mosses and the lichens. For no apparent reason, these casual patches of brilliant green thrive on the blackened bonfire ash.

We came here before the Clean Air Act and the sandstone on the Lodge, brick buildings and ancient tree trunks in the wood hardly supported the faintest tinge of green or quieter but attractive grey. Although we are more than twenty miles to the north-east of the industrial Black Country — and five or six miles as the crow flies from a power station — the air must have been heavy with smut. Sheep with grubby fleeces in the park next to us were suitable for the 'before' section of a washing powder advertisement. The air filters on the corn drier on the farm were frequently bunged up with soot.

Since those days all has changed. The sheep are now virginally white, the filters clean and, of far greater interest to me, a marvellous culture of lichens and mosses grows on the trees and in the wood. The trunks of the great oak trees outside my study window are a delicate green on the side that faces the prevailing wet south-western breeze. The sandstone birdbath which, in the old days, I vainly plastered with cowmuck to encourage greenery, is now a satisfying mellow tint, owing its complexion to progressive legislation. Fallen trees in the wood are soon clothed in a decent shroud of mosses, and lichens grow in unexpected places. It is a shining example that trying to stop the clock by preventing change does not work so well as more practical and progressive measures.

Nibbling away at the pines which threatened the remainder of our broad-leaved

The timber cut for sale to the garden-fencing trade

hardwoods with extinction worked fine – except that 'nibbling' was the operative word! In fact, fiddling would have been more accurate because, while I was messing about saving a few of the best individual native broad-leaved hardwoods, the rest of the pines were knitting their branches together into a thick enough canopy to stifle everything else.

Since I started making minor clearings round selected hardwood trees, there has been a major shift in government policy. Public pressure for preservation of what remains of our wildlife and rural amenities has swelled to proportions where any party that ignores it is threatened by a serious loss of votes. 'Green' issues have suddenly become the in-thing and the Forestry Commission, which has taken so much stick for years, is sensitive to such considerations. It is not really their fault that so many thousand acres are swathed in a dull monoculture of foreign softwood species, because they were planted in response to urgent demands to replace the forests devastated to help us win two wars. They have never been the vandals they were painted.

As long ago as 1949, the Forestry Commission planted Bagot's Wood, across the drive from us, with one row of oak trees in every three of pines, because it was originally a famous oakwood and was planted so that it would be an oakwood again when the present crop of pines was felled. But good news does not hit the headlines until such areas are designated as 'scientifically interesting', and therefore the wisdom and foresight in their creation is rarely credited to those who gave them birth. Having discovered, from personal experience, how helpful the Forestry is, I put my cards on the table and in the autumn of 1985 I asked the District Officer for his advice.

He was only recently appointed but he could see for himself that the crop of softwoods was mediocre, so I explained to him that my concern was not to make my fortune out of flogging pines but to leave the place better than it was when we arrived.

I wished it to revert to the broad-leaved native hardwoods which it is the policy of the Forestry to encourage, and I showed him, somewhat sheepishly, how oak and hornbeam had flourished where I had given space – without seeking his permission!

We walked the wood and the more minutely we inspected it, the longer his face grew. There was a tremendous lot of oak and birch and mountain ash, struggling to stand up in the pine-crush closing in around them, but he said that without *drastic* action their life expectancy was short. I would have to act fast or there would be no hardwoods to save.

I said that I would like to clear-fell the pines, leaving only the self-regenerated English trees that were fighting for survival, but the technical snag, from the licensing viewpoint, was that the pines were not mature and 'ripe' so did not qualify for clear-fell. He advised, instead, that I apply for a 'thinning' licence, because thinning can range anywhere from 'light' to 'heavy' and the decision which is which is subjective enough to allow scope for some difference of opinion!

So I slapped in a request for a licence to thin the whole lot over a period of five years. This would give me time to try various contractors and markets

A 'heavy' thin is a subjective term – but will make room for native broad-leaved trees in place of foreigners

to generate the maximum cash for other projects. Although I was very conscious of the urgency, I dared not allow more than one contractor in the wood at a time – and then out of the breeding season of birds and deer, because disturbance on more than one side may threaten to cut off the escape of wildlife and do irreparable damage by 'spooking' them.

The wood had been notified as part of the SSSI since 1968 – but such constructive advice about sacrificing softwoods for more important hardwoods does not appear to be part of Nature Conservancy duties. Because it *is* an SSSI, the Commission was legally bound to seek NCC reaction before issuing a licence. The NCC appear to have been too busy to confirm the licence speedily but, as the Commission had advised the thinning, I started to fell the first stand in order to catch the 1985 Christmas trade, months before the licence landed on my desk.

...rnbeam which is growing
...y now that the pines have
...cleared from around it

48. AMBASSADORS FOR WILDLIFE

Although our three pools are among my favourite spots, they might have a job to qualify as having been 'existing features' for very long. Primrose Dell is marked as a marl pit on the Ordnance Survey map so it was presumably dug out with picks and shovels by hairy-chested chaps who enriched the land with the marl they dug. How long ago that happened is anybody's guess, but perhaps in my grandfather's grandfather's time.

Middle Pool was made by us when the contractors who erected the deer fence dammed a ditch to give a straighter fenceline. Botanists now enthuse over the water soldiers I introduced – and I enjoy the dragonflies and newts which have colonised the plant life there.

Dunstal Pool, though far more impressive than either the 'pit-holes', still owes its origin to the artifice of Man. It was formed by throwing up a bank on the south side to dam the drainage from the wood, and was intended as a reservoir to supply two farms, downstream, with water.

At an acre and a half large, it is quite an impressive sheet of water situated just across the paddock from the sitting-room. When visitors arrive, it is the first thing which catches their eye because nothing enhances a view as much as water.

Wild duck stay well if baited with plenty of corn

Tufted duck are superb divers and feed on the water insects and tadpoles in Dunstan Pool

As soon as I curbed local shooters who poached every duck and goose which dared to show its bill upon the pool, I attracted a good variety of wildfowl as any keeper would have done. I hatched and reared a clutch of mallard under a bantam hen who brought them up around the house as tame as domestic ducks. I also persuaded them to stay, as any keeper would, by giving them enough wheat to eat to make it unnecessary for them to have to go elsewhere to satisfy their appetites.

The sight of these idle, well-fed duck, strutting safely around the paddock or swimming on the pool, attracted their wild relatives who were decoyed here by such luxury. By spreading a bucketful of wheat on the paddock and spilling a sackful of potatoes in the shallows, I had no difficulty in attracting mixed flocks of wildfowl up to a hundred strong.

Their breeding success was abysmal, though, because the water in the pool was clear as crystal but supported no water plants at all. When we had it analysed we discovered it was too acid for most plants to thrive and were advised to put limestone chippings in the ditch that fed it, to improve the alkalinity – with no effect at all.

Gerald Springthorpe and I collected trailer-loads of pondweed, as we had for Primrose Dell (*see* page 167), with no better results until, by dogged trial and error, not scientific know-how, we stumbled on a weedy pool with similar characteristics. Broad-leaved pondweed, water crowsfoot and wild yellow waterlilies at last took hold and formed a base for water boatmen, spiders, water beetles and a whole spectrum of beetles to breed to provide natural food for waterfowl.

We already had a good colony of toads and reasonable numbers of frogs and these bred enough tadpoles to attract a couple of pairs of tufted duck which nested on the island, but the explosion in insect life the new waterweed attracted brought resident little grebe, or dabchicks, which are by far my favourite waterfowl. They are only about as big as a man's clenched fist, round as little apples

– and the most spectacular divers it has been my pleasure to know. One second they are on the surface as buoyant as children's celluloid toy ducks, the next they plunge from view without causing so much as a ripple. They must have lungs as strong as diving bells because they stay submerged, swimming after prey, so long that I despair for their survival. Then they pop up like corks many yards away from where they submerged.

These little dabchicks are not rare and would never excite a twitcher. But they are shy, demanding seclusion, and if supplies of insect food and breeding cover are not to their liking, they simply go away. I am delighted to give them sanctuary – though I am the first to admit that their acceptance of my invitation owes more to luck than judgement.

Such projects are easier now because I stumbled on a specialist in messing about with water, someone who has forgotten more than I shall ever know. He is Jeremy Purseglove, landscape architect for the Severn–Trent Water Board.

In the past, Water Boards have taken as much flak as the Forestry Commission for vandalising the countryside so their officials might seem strange bedfellows for the likes of me – and vice versa, since I am not shy of criticising what I regard as the unhelpful activities of bureaucracy.

The River Blythe, which feeds Blithfield Reservoir, about three miles from me, is a delightful river which meanders a tortuous course through flowery water-meadows. Hearing that the Water Board was engaged on a 'flood prevention' scheme, I went along to see – and probably to criticise! Planting acres and acres

Yellow water-lilies

of boring pines got the Forestry Commission a bad name which sticks despite their improvements in technique. 'Flood prevention' was the comparable Achilles Heel of Water Boards, though it was the Ministry of Agriculture who were mainly to blame for advising (and subsidising) farmers to drain traditional water-meadows so that they could increase corn mountains instead of butter bogs. The Water Boards were the pigs-in-the-middle, rightly criticised for ripping out trees along the banks where otters made their holts, converting beautiful rivers to geometric drains, as unromantic as open sewers.

Jeremy Purseglove is trying to pick up the pieces for the Water Board just as Gerald Springthorpe has done for the Forestry Commission. Both are true ambassadors for wildlife.

The conventional method, until recently, was to drive a straight channel to cut off all the natural snaking of the river, leaving a drain as characterless as a conventional canal to sluice the water to the sea. Cut deep enough, it drained the surrounding meadows so that wildflowers could be ploughed in, as weeds, and trees uprooted to make way for corn

The principle I found at the River Blythe was just the same – but the technique was different. The Board had indeed cut a straight depression but, instead of being below the water level, it was wide and shallow and about a foot *above* the surface of the water.

In normal weather, the river meandered its leisurely way along the bed of the valley, finding Nature's easiest route, as it had done for centuries. The same trees studded the banks that had studded it before and, to top it off, Jeremy Purseglove had sown the channel he had cut with wildflower seed to spread into the water-meadows. In times of storm and flood, when the river level rose more than a foot, the surplus was deflected down the new channel, as flooded rivers streamed down the bed of ancient water-meadows. It was a highly practical compromise, which both prevented major flooding and preserved the character of the river at the same time.

It is a rare pleasure to discover bureaucrats brave enough to cock a snook at conventions and practices peddled by the dogma of their fellows, so I was delighted to arrange a return visit round my reserve.

His scientific but highly practical experience was rich with suggestions about how and where to improve the flora and wildlife in my pools. The water I've encouraged to flow into Primrose Dell (*see* page 168) will obviously be vastly different from the acid drainage over woodland peat because the water flows, instead, over the intensively farmed plough of an ultra-modern farm, and will be full of surplus nitrates and artificial fertiliser.

But that is precisely the problem that will face so many folk who try to make the best of little pools, left in odd corners by farmers who are doing what they can to aid conservation as well as make a living in an unfriendly world. Left to myself, I should have to flounder twixt trial and error, trying first this plant, then that. So I am hoping that Jeremy Purseglove's advice will short-circuit some of my problems and that, in turn, I can supply material for a few unorthodox experiments.

49. FOX-TROT

As I described on page 137, we made the mistake of placing the artificial House Sett behind a clump of rhododendrons, out of view of the sitting-room windows, and as the woodland edge is just over the ditch, the badgers can emerge and disappear into cover, on the lightest summer night, without us being any the wiser.

So I decided to offer alternative accommodation where we should benefit as much as they did. I decided to cash in on the saw-pit we had filled with tree roots when we made the deer glade (*see* page 117). Badgers love excavating the soil between a jumble of tree roots because they can then site their den in dry security under some great root – but they do like a tunnel entrance.

A local firm makes the great concrete pipes often used in road construction as culverts or pipes to divert streams or transfer sewage. I discovered that scrap or damaged pipes are sometimes sold off cheap when their flanges will not fit or some other defect prevents them from being used for their original purpose. So I bought enough to make a tunnel about thirty yards long and waited for the next time Bill Durose turned up with his JCB digger. He is self-employed and when he has a slack patch, he drops in to see if there are any fill-in jobs

There are always foxes in our heavily wooded area

(to be paid for out of Christmas trees!). Because this is a mutually beneficial arrangement, his price is *very* competitive. I asked him to make a curving trench, sloping down towards the water's edge, with one end in the bank above the pool and the other leading from the root pile we had already covered, and two ends of the trench were carefully sited where there was an unobstructed view of them from both the study and sitting-room windows.

All that remained was to roll the concrete pipes, which were twelve inches in diameter, into the trench and cover them with the soil we had excavated when the trench was dug. As they were buried we were able to arrange them — in much the same way as we reconstructed the artificial sett in Primrose Dell — so that there was enough space between each pair of pipes for a badger to start a whole series of side tunnels to make the sort of labyrinth badgers love so much.

The sett was not initially a howling success. Rabbits took to it at once and apparently made a warren among the tree roots, constructing several unplanned entrances as well as using the tunnel we had made. Footprints in the mud indicated that badgers paid occasional visits of inspection, but there were no signs of bedding being taken in, so it seemed unlikely that they had actually taken up residence.

Then, at the end of the following March, fairly regular sightings of a vixen roused our suspicion that she was interested in more than rabbit for supper. We saw her morning and evening, several times a week, either entering or leaving the carefully sited entrances to the 'badger sett'. It raised a very tricky problem concerning my relationship with Andy, the local keeper, because our gentleman's agreement was that he would damage neither hawks nor owls nor, above all, badgers, in exchange for which I would not harbour foxes which were really the only predators to be a serious threat to his stock of game. His chicks and poults were safe in rearing pens, but no one could deny that wild pheasants, when they had laid their clutch of eggs, and partridge and wild duck, were all on the fox's menu.

Every year, therefore, when I spotted a vixen and cubs, I kept my side of the bargain by allowing Andy to deal with them. I always felt slightly guilty about it because foxes did the wildlife in my reserve very little harm indeed and, on the credit side, they killed scores of rabbits which would otherwise have played hell with neighbouring farmers' crops.

I was therefore between two stools. On the one hand, I felt duty-bound to sign the vixen's death warrant by telling Andy. On the other, I persuaded myself there was so much easy grub in my wood, in the shape of rabbits, that she would not need to stray so far as to put his game at risk. In the end I told him but said that if he did not feel too strongly about it, I should be grateful if he would give her the benefit of the doubt and leave her alone so long as she did not hunt on his beat. Our relationship was such that he had no hesitation about agreeing. As a result, Jess and I enjoyed entertainment for several weeks that money wouldn't buy. From 5 April until the end of June, we 'fox-watched' every evening from the comfort of our own armchairs.

At about half past five, the vixen emerged from the earth, had a jolly good scratch — and quietly surveyed the scene.

Many would be surprised to learn that, sharing the root-pile with the foxes was a warrenful of rabbits. Perhaps they chose subterranean tunnels which were too narrow for a fox to penetrate and follow them to the fastness of their burrows. The rabbits grazed fairly near their warren from mid afternoon, and one old warrior — it is impossible to know which sex — would move to within four or five feet of the main entrance, ears cocked like a pair of radar scanners, as it listened in for sounds of vulpine movement underground. When the vixen emerged, this rabbit showed absolutely no sign of panic, merely moving quietly back another yard or so.

When the vixen had been out surveying her surroundings for five or ten minutes, the cubs emerged, apparently spontaneously as there was no visible sign from the vixen, and we were too far away to hear if she made any sound.

For a week or so, the cubs sunned themselves in the evening sun and played a little round the mouth of the hole. The 'sentry' rabbit kept vigil, with no sign of nerves, and six or eight others from the same warren continued grazing as if they hadn't a care in the world. When the vixen thought it time to go off on her hunting foray, she must have given some signal we could not detect, because the cubs went to ground, as if on command.

The vixen then set off across the deer glade, towards the wood, and fifteen or twenty rabbits grazing there scarcely troubled to hop half a dozen yards out of her way. There was no sign at all of the panic one expects prey to have in

The rabbits appear quite happy
to feed close to the fox's earth

the presence of their predators and there is absolutely no doubt in my mind that the rabbits *knew* the vixen was not hunting and did not have *them* or her menu for the family's supper.

It reminded me of the old country belief that 'foxes do not catch hens near their own earth'. I may say, in passing, that my hens were several hundred yards away — and she *did* catch five of them, which I took as poor gratitude for my tolerance and hospitality, though I concede that they were not as near her earth as the immune rabbits were!

As the cubs grew older and bolder, they enlarged their play area and chased each other in rough-and-tumble mock battles and Chase-me-Charlie frolics over an area as big as a tennis court, and it was quite amazing to see fox cubs and rabbits often playing simultaneously in different-sized concentric circles. Still the rabbits showed no fear, and several times indulged in chasing games of their own outside the area which the cubs monopolised, but within easy striking distance of the vixen. The vixen was hunting farther afield and regularly returned with rabbits she had caught in the wood or on the far side of the deer glade, which the cubs tore up and devoured voraciously.

At the end of June, the vixen moved the whole litter into surrounding fields of standing corn. It was a perfect demonstration of the unexpected tolerance between hunters and the hunted — perhaps because local prey may be spared instinctively in case they are needed for an unexpected rainy day?

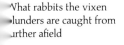

What rabbits the vixen plunders are caught from further afield

50. FROM FEG TO FERTILITY

Strangers going up the drive that borders Holly Covert might think that one world has ended and the next has begun when they cross the cattle-grid at the top of Daffodil Lawn. Gone are the days when Bagot's Park was famous for its goats and deer, its ancient oaks and chestnuts, and infamous for its decrepit stag-headed trees and profitless rush and feggy grass. The goats have now been rescued by the Rare Breeds Survival Trust and the deer are no longer as welcome as they were when there was only rough park and scrubland to be grazed. The unproductive waste has been cultivated into a productive farm of almost a thousand acres. Farming 'enterprise' would be the modern term, and this describes it aptly because about half the land is down to corn and rape while a thousand sheep add organic muck and profit to the rest. They no longer paddle round all winter in the cloying heavy clay but are comfortably straw-bedded in a covered yard. There could be no contrast starker than this example of intensive husbandry, as modern as tomorrow, and my attempts to maintain enough 'natural' woodland habitat for the benefit of the birds and bees.

David Core is the efficient farm manager and, on our records, it might seem that we have nothing at all in common. Wise neighbours in the country bend over backwards to get on because so many adjacent farmers fall out over straying stock or bad hedges, blocked drains and disputed boundaries, that sensible countrymen take effective action before it is too late. Arm's-length politeness is an effective general rule because those who meet least often have least time to fall out. But, despite being at opposite ends of the rural spectrum, David Core and I get on fine. If I need anything shifted, heavier than my little Fergie tractor will pull, or if one of my implements gets stuck, I can always rely on a cheerful response from David with one of the great four-wheel-drive juggernauts he uses as normal workhorses. If he wants some logs, he can always use my chain-saw and he goes down to the village every morning to fetch his post and papers – and drops off the mail to his neighbours on the way back.

Our greatest mutual benefit is the grazing on Daffodil Lawn. When we arrived, the colony of wild daffs was meagre because of damage by trespassers – and even more damage by the chain-harrow used to destroy the blooms. I stopped the trespassers easily enough but the daffs would have perished unless a crop of grass was taken off as hay or by grazing, because an uncut crop of brittle feg would have stifled the next season's growth.

So we have a scheme that suits us both. David takes a crop of hay – but not till the daffs have flowered and seeded. Then he grazes the turf short until about the end of August when he puts on some rich organic muck, taken from his sheepyard, to ensure a bounteous crop of grass the following year. He avoids covering areas where the daffodils thrive because 'strong' organic muck might scorch them.

Sheep and deer carry some of the same internal parasites so I let the meadow lie fallow and ungrazed for a couple of months after the sheep have gone, to break the life cycle of any parasites the sheep have dropped. This is more vital for me than for him because he can catch up his sheep and drench or inject them against worms or flukes but I cannot catch up the deer to dose them.

When the grass is clean again, about the beginning of November, I open the gate from the wood and let the deer onto the lawn. They have, by then, taken as much as I want (or more!) from the wood so that productive grazing of the well-managed turf carries them over winter. When they are thoroughly accustomed to going up there nightly, I can put the deer crush into operation and control their numbers humanely (*see* page 165).

As soon as tiny daffodil shoots show through in early spring, the deer are locked out again, to let the daffs flower and seed and spread to their golden hearts' delight.

This is a neat example of friendly give-and-take, which has advantages for both me and David.

Living a mile from the main road, our water supply is piped over Edward Froggatt's (another neighbour's) land, to supply both him and our joint neighbour, Trevor Jolliffe. This is another source of potential wrangles because when the supply was first installed, the land which the three of us now own all belonged to the same landowner who was doing his tenants a favour by forking out the cash to lay the pipes. If any of them grumbled, he could bang their heads together or tell them to find another farm.

An ancient lady lived alone in the Lodge in those days, and the one stark cold tap could have encouraged her to use water for little but brewing endless cups of tea over her open fire. The farmers, predecessors of my present neighbours, each milked about twenty cows which had access to a stream to drink, and the

neighbour's sheep keep
…odil Lawn in good heart

David Core is a tower of strength and an excellent neighbour

cows were hand-milked into buckets the contents of which were tipped into churns. The new water supply must have been a boon and a blessing – and he would have been a churlish lout who looked such a gift horse in the mouth.

Things have changed since then. The Froggatts and the Jolliffes bought their farms and they each have three sons. For five to make a living off a farm of well under two hundred acres leaves little scope for messing about. They both installed up-to-the-minute milking parlours, with machines to pump the milk directly through pipelines into tanks, and each farm milks more than a hundred cows.

Since milk is composed mostly of water, the actual amount drunk daily by the cows is obviously at least five times as much as it was when I came. Add to that the fact that there is an incentive on cleanliness, and pipelines and tanks need far more water to wash them than the pails they have replaced, and there is no need to have been sired by Einstein to calculate that the consumption of water through our joint pipe has escalated out of all proportion. It is largely a dairy-farming area, having some of the best grassland in the country, and the other farms further afield have increased water consumption proportionately.

We gradually noticed that, when the two farms between us and the water main on the road were milking, our cold tap stopped running. It stopped when 200 cows all went to their water troughs to stock up for the next stint of milk production – and it stopped again when the dairymen swilled down.

On some days, our cold tap – the only input to the storage tank in the roof – stopped running for five or more hours. The washing machine didn't work for several hours a day and nor did the dishwasher. We couldn't have a bath, except when nobody was milking or swilling down, or when the cows weren't drinking in unison!

We got fed up with it – and I gave it so much adverse publicity that the water company eventually admitted that demand had outstripped supply and they put in a mechanical booster so we now get all the water we need.

But where do we get it from? The pools in our wood have a low water level in every piffling dry spell. The Story Brook, which runs through Bagot's Park, was almost dry for the first time in living memory in 1985 – which we all thought was an exceptionally wet summer. David Core has kept accurate records of rainfall *every day* for many years, and the graph shows that, although we did have an exceptional number of days in 1985 when some rain fell, the total for the year was five to seven inches less than in 1980, '81 and '82. It was also less than 1983 and '84, to our great surprise.

Therefore, although there is little doubt that 1985 was *not* as wet as it was painted, the water level in our pools was critical and suggests that demand for water is exceeding supply in more than our locality which may have ill effects not only on farming but on wildlife conservation. Just as gas-guzzling cars threaten the finite supplies of vital oil, it seems to me that good housekeeping with precious water is just as vital. Add to this the fact that surplus nitrogen from modern intensive farming threatens pollution of what streams do still run, and it is obvious that effective action is absolutely vital.

51. SELF SUFFICIENT

I have always been fascinated by livestock. I kept my first tame rabbit when I was seven, and my first ferret — to bolt wild rabbits into purse nets, or rats for my terrier — a couple of years later. We always kept poultry, killed a pig for the good of the table, and my father kept a couple of Jersey house cows as a hobby.

Jess's family were much the same, and they had a pony and trap and pigeons and rabbits, as pets for the children, while the breakfast eggs were new laid from free-range hens. When we were first married, we scrounged eggs and butter from our families for a year or so until we got a house where we could keep livestock of our own.

Never having bought a 'shop' egg in her life, it followed that Jess brought our hens, ducks and pigeons with us when we came to the Lodge. So, whatever the weather, my first chore is to feed the stock, and I have wandered round on

The wild Canada geese with their substitute brood, later to become our Christmas dinner

icy mornings cold enough to make the handle of the bucket stick to my fingers with frost. Ruth mucks in too – and a very practical country girl she is. When she and her sister bottle-reared a couple of cade lambs, they called them Deep and Freeze!

Naturalist skills and stockmanship are closely entwined because conservation – as opposed to preservation – is an unsentimental, earthy effort to ensure that both wild and tame creatures have the right conditions for a dignified and natural life so that, when the time comes, there is no reluctance to treat them as a crop.

My interests are more involved with the fauna on the reserve than with the flora. Jess, who is also actively interested in everything that goes on out in the wood, is even more in tune with her garden. When pressures build up, she releases the tension by escaping to plant or weed, reap or prune her beloved flowers and shrubs. The instant cure for a threat of depression is to feel the fertile soil sifting through her fingers. I am not particularly fond of roses, which I regard as ungrateful, prickly brutes, hiding their aggressive spite under deceptively per-fumed beautiful flowers, but Jess walks round morning, evening and odd times in between, until she knows each bloom on every bush.

She prefers her flowers and shrubs to be fragrant, not only for her own delight but to attract honey bees and flamboyant butterflies to share her pleasure. Sweet-scented viburnums and azaleas, and lilies-of-the-valley are the sort of plants she loves, and she panders to the vices of bumble bees by encouraging them to get drunk on the nectar of her sedums and michaelmas daisies.

Ruth collecting the eggs

We buy a dozen and a half day-old cock chicks every March – and they are pretty lucky birds. We buy from a chap who breeds tens of thousands of broiler chicks, intensively reared so that they can be slaughtered when about ten weeks old, for the chicken-in-the-basket trade. We don't keep ours in a foetid shed, lit by artificial light and fed on scientifically-formulated pellets which make them grow so fast their flesh has less texture and flavour than soggy cotton wool.

Our cock chicks have the freedom of the spinney which runs all along one side of the paddock from the garden to the pool. They are fed on sound wheat, have all the grass they want and freedom to scratch for insects as their wild ancestors did before they were domesticated. They don't grow nearly as fast as intensively kept broilers do – but we are after quality at the expense of quantity. They run on, under these free-range, natural conditions, for about seven months by which time they weigh about twelve pounds and are as big as small turkeys – and far more succulent. They have natural, happy lives and we put about two-thirds in the deep freeze and give the rest away to friends for Christmas.

The Canada geese nest on the island in the pool and, when they have completed their full clutch of eggs, I swap them for the same number of domestic goose eggs. The wild birds never notice and continue to sit, incubating and then rearing the domestic goslings as if they were their own. In July, the Canadas fly away to join the other wild geese, in flocks on reservoirs and lakes, but their 'offspring' are too heavy to get airborne so stay with us to form the basis of our Christmas dinner or the focus of a party for our friends.

My interest in the pheasants is really a marriage between the arts of naturalist and stockman. I feed them all season in a 'gravity' feeder hung from a tree branch about twenty yards from my study window. It is a very simple contraption, consisting of an old five-gallon oil drum which had been thoroughly cleaned and then had slots about a quarter of an inch wide punched in the bottom. It is then filled with wheat, or other grain, and suspended so that the slots are about a foot above the ground. The corn in the drum jams in the slots so that it doesn't trickle out until disturbed.

The pheasants tumble to the knack of working their automatic dispensing canteen surprisingly quickly – I always rate them as exceptionally unintelligent. But they soon discover that if they peck at the grain they can see jammed in a slot, an eggcupful or so trickles out before it jams again. So the routine is one peck to disturb the grain, and there is an eggcupful or so on the ground to be scoffed before the next brain-bending effort of pecking the right spot to release some more. It is a most effective way of selective feeding which I also use for the laying hens and table cockerels because it means that I can be away for a day, confident that the stock will not go hungry.

If the drums are hung as high as pheasants and domestic stock can reach, they will be too high to be raided by jackdaws and sparrows. At the same time, well-fed stock is usually too idle to search out every odd grain in the litter below the drum so that there is always enough to attract a few chaffinches, green linnets and yellowhammers which adds interest and movement to the farmyard scene.

The cock pheasants give a lovely splash of colour to the sward in front of the windows but, as breeding time approaches, they harry the hens and fight among themselves so much that good stockmanship demands the cocks be reduced to about one to five or seven hens. Entirely for their own good, of course!

od pigeons learn to use the
ity grain-feeder put out for
sants

52. ONE MAN'S MEAT

It is difficult to appreciate just what conflicts there are over every scrap of habitat, even among those who profess the common cause of conservation. At one end of the scale are the Look Alikes, the academic purists who worship at the shrine of rarity, fighting futile campaigns to stop the unstoppable. Males of the species wear earnest expressions — and usually beards — and the females would also fit the description Look Alike, except that they are (usually) less hairy.

When such people visit our wood, they drool about the heronry because, they say, it is 'important' and contains 1% of all the herons' nests in the country, but they scarcely take a second glance at the badger setts because badgers are 'common'.

I occupy the humblest rung on the ladder because, however common they still may be, I believe badgers are under a far greater threat than herons. Some of the circumstantial mud thrown by the Ministry of Agriculture pseudoscientists, obsessed by bovine TB, was bound to stick. The result has been an upsurge in the obscene 'sports' of badger digging and badger baiting. So I put a far greater value on experiments I have done to persuade wild badgers to occupy my 'undigg-able' root-and-pipe setts than on a more spectacular increase in the number of nests in the heronry.

Visiting Look Alikes criticise the deer because they say that the deer nip out a great deal of regeneration that might create the thickets in which I want to harbour a greater variety of species. They are, of course, quite right. Fallow deer are great browsers, not content with grazing grass as more civilised domestic stock might be.

When scots pine are felled, the deer bark at the tender top ends of the trunks

One of my great pleasures — observing wild fallow deer at close quarters

But every visionary needs a catalyst to spark his enthusiasm from theory to practice, and dawn expeditions to watch deer made me fall in love with them. My two greatest thrills when we bought the wood were being able to observe wild deer and wild badgers on my own land. As time went on and I got to know our deer as individuals, my visual pleasure was spurred by the protective urge aroused when foxhounds pulled one down before my eyes.

So I am prepared to sacrifice a few young hazels (which would have cosseted more grey squirrels!) and a few rare birds, which might have nested in denser cover, for the sake of the deer which inspired me to find sanctuary in the first place. That does not mean that I am starry-eyed to the point of sentimentality, for it is *I* who urges Gerald to take a heavier annual cull so that the survivors do not wreak unacceptable havoc – and I am practical enough to have no qualms about enjoying the venison provided by the victims of our management control!

Having said that, we should by no means achieve perfection if we exterminated the deer completely. I tried an interesting experiment by fencing a square of twenty yards by twenty with wire netting of large enough mesh to exclude deer but nothing smaller. Inside the compound, I put another fence of small enough mesh to exclude rabbits but not mice and voles. And, finally, a small enclosure that even excluded mice.

It was therefore possible to assess what damage was done by deer and rabbits and mice; what was done by rabbits and mice but not deer; what was done by mice alone; and, finally, what plants would survive with complete protection from such predators. The results showed that rabbits were by far the most destructive and that getting rid of *all* the deer would do little good unless all the rabbits were also despatched.

Where self-set hawthorn and blackthorn appear, the deer may browse their tender shoots so that, although they may well be late developers, their twigs and branches grow as dense as a lovingly barbered hedge, and this makes ideal

Rabbits bark and kill
regenerating hawthorn

nesting sites for birds. But, if rabbits take a shine to the same bush, they ring-bark the main stem and kill it.

The most dedicated specialist botanists are like 'twitchers' in the feathered world. A twitcher is the lowest form of ornithological life whose sole object is to tick off the names of birds seen against a catalogue of every species which might possibly visit the areas that he covers. These people are mere collectors who vie with each other for the highest number of different birds observed, in the same way that schoolkids collect foreign stamps or film stars' autographs.

Botanist twitchers start off with a map divided into 20-kilometre squares and spend their free time making a complete inventory of species of plant which grow there. He who produces the most impressive, but verifiable, list, tops the esteem of his fellows. I have a certain sympathy with these botanists who have spent years compiling catalogues of the whereabouts of plants and flowers and who get narrow-minded when they return to find species they never saw last time which have been transplanted by others. But chemical herbicides are now so widely used that it seems sensible to transfer almost any insect or plant which will find the wood congenial.

A great bone of contention is the question of public access. It is perfectly natural for lovers of wildlife to wish to see their favourite species. The snag is that the modern trend of increased leisure (voluntary, or enforced by labour-saving machines) means that more and more people have time to kill. Leisure is the major growth industry so that the same mass of people wish to converge on what was once quiet countryside.

Government grants towards nature reserves and SSSIs obviously come from taxes, and those who pay taxes also have votes. So a powerful lobby says that money should not be 'squandered' on wildlife unless the man that pays the piper can call the tune by having access to enjoy the birds and beasts he subsidises. Shy creatures do not agree. The copybook example is the otter which has declined in recent years to become an endangered species, not least because of disturbance by fishermen and boaters and walkers on river banks where it needs seclusion to survive. Among the great advantages of reserves like mine, which are not parasitic on the public purse, is that their owners can decide who visits them.

The herons' nests in our wood have greatly increased mainly because the birds are not disturbed while they are breeding, either by me but far less by twitchers and the like. Left to themselves, they are capable of dealing with their natural predators. By operating the reserve as a sanctuary for birds, rather than for bird-watchers, it has been possible to produce a surplus which can overspill for others to enjoy without destroying the vital sense of security. If that sounds to be inhospitable to fellow voters, I make no apology.

53. EXPERIMENT AND ENCOURAGE

The public's reaction to wildlife is totally illogical. When foxhounds meet on Boxing Day, the Master is liable to have a thunderflash tied to his nag's tail because 'foxhunting is cruel, and it is wrong to enjoy it'. If I join the local ferret and terrier boys for a good day's ratting – which I thoroughly enjoy – no one raises an eyebrow. But I doubt if rats or foxes – or even noble stags – would draw much distinction.

Gerald Springthorpe, who has been conserving wildlife on Forestry Commission land for years, is showered with praise if he erects an observation tower from which the public can watch wild deer, but only a tiny minority is interested if he persuades the local forester to leave suitable areas unplanted so that adders and lizards, which have lived there for centuries, can continue to breed and thrive. Yet snakes and lizards are threatened far more by loss of habitat when large areas are suddenly shaded by trees than are deer, which are mobile enough to find another feeding ground.

Two of the most delightful creatures I have ever had were a stoat and a weasel which I had reared (at different times) and both were tame enough to live in the house. Yet the publisher I was working for at the time fell out with me irreparably because I insisted on calling the book *A Weasel in My Meatsafe* (which was where he lived as a kitten). The publisher said that 'the public don't like weasels, so the title will put them off'. I am glad to say he was wrong and the book did very well when it came out under another imprint, and also when it was re-issued by Michael Joseph in 1977.

As a child, I spent countless happy hours catching newts in the local 'swags' – which were pools formed by mining subsidence. My mother was a tolerant woman and, in spring, we kept an aquarium of breeding newts in the centre of the breakfast table and I marvelled at the sinuous yellow-bellied grace of the male crested newts in May. They were then so common that once, when I forgot to fix the lid on the aquarium, twenty escaped all over the house and turned up in the most unlikely places for weeks afterwards. Now they are so rare that they have been added to the list of protected species under the Wildlife and Countryside Act, and it is an offence to catch one.

It so happens that I know an old army camp where, although demolished when the war was over, the bases of some buildings were water-proofed and left standing as firefighting reservoirs in case the adjacent woodland was ignited. Although a chain of these reservoirs was sited within a few hundred yards, some were colonised by smooth newts and others by crested newts and, so far as we could tell, the species kept to separate tanks, for no reason that I have ever been able to establish.

I caught numbers of the crested species (I repeat, which now would be an offence under the Wildlife and Countryside Act) and put them in Primrose Dell just before they were ready to spawn at the end of April. The experiment was a flop because the herons found them almost immediately and ranged themselves

round the pool in a circle like coarse fishermen in a Sunday contest. As the newts surfaced to take in a fresh supply of air, the herons knocked them off. I knew then how fishermen, who whinge about my herons, must feel when they send me letters of complaint about their trout being taken.

Sadly, most of the grass snakes I swapped for a breeding colony of harvest mice (*see* page 156) suffered almost the same fate for, to a heron's eyes, I suppose a grass snake looks much like a succulent eel. A few survivors fetched up in the compost heap in a neighbour's garden but some moved diagonally across the wood, settling at the corner of Dunstal Pool where it meets the paddock. So I dumped a few barrowfuls of lawn mowings close by and when they heated up and the surface was warm, the grass snakes coiled up there in a writhing cat's-cradle, drinking in the sun. One old matriarch was over three feet long and, though prissy women feigned fits of the dreaded shudders, most folk who saw them found them utterly delightful.

I have had great pleasure from the muntjac deer which are non-native 'introductions' by any standards and are rather frowned on by the Forestry Commission who object to them fraying young trees. They were introduced about the turn of the century by the same Duke of Bedford who also introduced grey squirrels. Escapees from the ducal park at Woburn, mainly after the last war, have been colonising the country, spreading about twenty miles further from Woburn each year. This is because they love dense cover, but are natural wanderers and therefore find crops of standing corn or hay ideal sanctuary. They are only about the size of a fox – indeed, they are very foxy coloured and could easily be mistaken for one as they creep through thickets.

I have already mentioned my rhododendrons which are severely frowned on by conventional conservationists who complain they are not native to our shores.

Crested newts are now so rare that they have been given legal protection

hand-reared stoat which
d two litters

Nor are many other things, including rabbits and Spanish chestnut, but they are none the worse for that, though I do stick to native species where possible and only introduced the rhododendrons to outwit the maverick keeper next door.

But the whole point of a reserve like mine is to encourage the maximum variety of native species and to experiment with them to discover which are adaptable enough to thrive. I really don't see much difference between that and putting up artificial nesting boxes to encourage a greater variety of birds to breed here than would ever have done so naturally. Both enhance the chances of a wider spectrum of wildlife thriving.

54. THE SYSTEM

Having spent four fruitless years trying to discover the NCC guidelines for selection of sites they intend to schedule, my frustration blew its top.

The main purpose of this book is to encourage all with sympathy for wildlife under pressure to take action, on however small a scale, to improve or conserve habitat. This can be done with or without the Nature Conservancy Council's help.

I have enjoyed half a lifetime in just such a labour of love and have maintained close contact with the Regional Officer of the Conservancy who has been a frequent visitor to my reserve and knows precisely what I do. Repeated pleas to get his review completed in time to be recorded for this book brought no results, so I lit a fuse that never fails to spark life into the most reluctant bureaucrat. I wrote to the Top of the Tree in July 1985.

William Waldegrave, Minister of State for the Environment, Countryside and Local Government, is a rising star in the political firmament who does not let grass grow under his or any subordinate's feet if he can help it. His co-operative reply had the desired effect of producing a letter in November from the Regional Officer saying that consideration of my SSSI had been given 'some priority'. If it takes letters to a Secretary of State to engender action to help those who are demonstrably passionate conservationists, I shudder to think what happens to less committed − or persistent − owners of potentially valuable sites for wildlife.

In December, the Assistant Regional Officer appeared and introduced himself as Mark July. Pronounced Julie. Although he was knowledgeable and helpful, he would not divulge the criteria on which selection of SSSIs depends because, he said, it was a confidential in-house document which was not revealed to the general public. A small voice whispered that Big Brother knows best.

We walked round the wood and, when we returned to my study, he produced three pages of closely typed foolscap entitled *Operations Likely to Damage the Features of Special Scientific Interest.* It was a checklist, from which he proceeded to enumerate the sort of things a Management Agreement might specify or forbid.

It appeared to have been drawn up by some boffin to ensure *complete* control of any land he cared to designate. This bureaucratic red tape-worm must have spent hours, at taxpayers' expense, composing his horror comic. The types of operation it listed ranged from cultivation, including ploughing, harrowing, rotovating and reseeding, to grazing (where damaging) and the introduction of grazing (where applicable). It reserved the right to prohibit changes in grazing regime (including type of stock or intensity or seasonal pattern or cessation of grazing). There were similar exhaustive provisos for mowing, fertilising, liming, releasing feral animals or plants and killing or removing any wild animal, including pest control. The list rabbited on *ad nauseam* until the small print in a cut-price insurance policy was concise by comparison.

I asked Mr July what sort of constraints might apply if we did strike up a Management Agreement, as would be necessary if the site were renotified. He said that it might be forbidden to spread straw on rides to feed pheasants if

and his gun – the model
keeper

their scratching for grain might damage the flora – just the sort of clause which would guarantee regurgitation by landowners who have retained copses and spinneys, uneconomic for agriculture but ideal for game! Despite slurs by anti-sporting interests, such owners value the wildlife as well as the game on their land, and generally are delighted to co-operate in *conservation* of wildlife as well. But co-operation cuts both ways, and conservation on private land cannot work without the active support of the owner.

Imagine the reaction of an independent countryman, who is genuinely trying to help, when some academic Look Alike threatens to take him to court for feeding his own pheasants! I felt the same, so Mr July and I parted rather stiffly.

The next episode in the saga was when I received the copy of the letter from the NCC to the Forestry Commission at the end of January 1986 about my application for a thinning licence to give room for native hardwoods (*see* page 185). It informed the Commission that the half of my wood then under discussion would not be renotified. I was bemused, to say the least, that they did not have the courtesy to send me written confirmation or denial of information about *my* land which, however, they had seen fit to supply to someone else.

When Mr July called again and I reminded him of his threat to prosecute me for feeding my own pheasants, he complained that I was twisting his words. Unaccustomed to being accused of not talking straight, I reached for my tape recorder and placed it on the desk between us. He was obviously taken aback but I explained that I had no wish to misquote him so that, if we recorded what we said, and either felt misjudged, we could replay the tape and settle the matter factually.

I felt like an old-fashioned lepidopterist, transfixing a struggling butterfly with a remorseless pin. We had an unpleasant half-hour's discussion during which it grew apparent that I had the wrong butterfly spiked to my specimen board. I had caught a common cabbage white, while the real villain was a backroom bumblecrat, cocooned in the cosy anonymity of an office at administrative headquarters.

The speculation was confirmed when my visitor produced an agreement from the recesses of his official briefcase. It was already drawn up and ready for me to sign. It specified, amongst other things, that I could let out three pigs in Holly Covert in the autumn, and even how many loads of leaf-mould I could remove from the wood for Jess's garden. Since the only reason that has ever been given for scheduling Holly Covert in the first place was the heronry, in the tree tops, it is difficult to see the relevance of either pigs or leaf-mould! To add insult to injury, the new agreement only covered Holly Covert and Daffodil Lawn, adding substance to my suspicion that the original lad I had taken for a grockle, who made the first visitation in 1982, had been briefed to reduce existing SSSIs. If I had signed the agreement, as I was requested, half the reserve would have been denotified. I therefore suggested to Mr July, in robust and basic natural history language, what he should do with his agreement.

Such bureaucratic arrogance alienates naturalists who are deeply committed to conservation and this episode should be a warning that no one should *ever* take the NCC at face value. The whole affair raised a principle far more important than anything to do with my small and unimportant wood. It is vital that the NCC Director General should cause the criteria his officials use to be made available for inspection. They must abide and work by the principle that protection will only work with active co-operation of those who own or live upon the land.

I have been extremely – and they may think unfairly – critical of our regional NCC staff, both for filibustering about decisions of any sort and for making contradictory statements which destroyed all trust in their integrity or competence.

To test my point, I wrote to the Chief Press Officer of the NCC, asking for any available literature on SSSIs and for clear official guidelines on the criteria they used. He replied that all literature had been withdrawn except for a leaflet he enclosed. It was entirely superficial. He passed the query about criteria to the Land Use Policy Branch – who I suspect are the niggers in the woodpile, and use regional staff to carry their cans. Their letter was a superb example of vintage gobbledegook, the only intelligible sentence being that 'the final decision on which land to notify rests with our Council'. Small fry, like the chaps who own the land, are presumably too far beneath contempt to take into their confidence.

So perhaps I had misjudged the Regional Officer and his understudy. The inoffensive Mr July apparently had no authority to make up his mind on anything not enmeshed in the web of red tape which binds up the 'operations likely to damage the special interest'. Like poor Sister Anna, who always carries the banner, he was stuck at the sharp end of negotiations to persuade the unwary to sign one of his agreements.

Perhaps it is not the small fry out in the regions who need livening up, though a basic course in public relations would do them no harm. It is the Big Fish at headquarters who need chivvying out of their cosy little pools to learn what really goes on in the great wide world outside. They would then discover, as gentle July did, that enthusiasm for conservation is not synonymous with being an easy pushover. NCC officers can only visit reserves and SSSIs occasionally – and not even then if not welcome because they have no automatic legal power of entry. This means they cannot necessarily monitor what goes on, whilst the owner is there twenty-four hours a day and can more or less do as he likes 'because what the eye doesn't see, the heart doesn't grieve about'.

In other words, no scheduled site or nature reserve can prosper without the willing co-operation of the landowner, especially one who will not submit to being treated like a juvenile delinquent whose IQ is not high enough to discuss the criteria by which the land he may love is judged.

The least the government should do is to treat those who are willing to co-operate as intelligent enough to be trusted with the facts so that they can participate in decisions that concern them, and even make original suggestions that have not occurred to the boffins. Until the NCC concedes this, my advice to any landowner asked to sign an agreement for the management of his land is to read the small print and sign *nothing* until the criteria on which the decision was based have been made available.

On 20 February 1986, a month after the Forestry Commission had been

Looking back from the Deer Glade, across the Dunstal Pool to the Lodge and Holly Covert

informed that the area they had originally leased, which is the part I am returning to broad-leaved trees, was not to be renotified as an SSSI, Mr July at last wrote to tell me himself. By this time, Daffodil Lawn, which the Regional Officer had repeatedly claimed was the best colony of wild daffs in the county, was also omitted; only the heronry in Holly Covert was included. It emphasised just how incompetent previous statements had been, and confirmed my decision that, if I ever did sign an agreement giving the Conservancy a say on my management committee of one – thus making it a committee of two – I should take adequate steps to make sure that the chairman still had the casting vote!

55. STEPPING STONES

Recent changes in the countryside have produced such rapid and fundamental effects that wildlife just cannot keep up. Evolution, to cope with them, would take millennia or centuries, not decades. It is therefore vital to try to protect some habitat which may be irreplaceable, and to replace other sites which are changing by providing similar habitat elsewhere. Neither is possible without either the willing co-operation or coercion of owners and farmers who live on the land.

There are a number of priorities involved in the task, ranging from threatened sites which are genuinely irreplaceable, to management of marginally important sites which could be improved to become new reservoirs of wildlife. Top priority are wetland sites where draining and subsequent ploughing would obviously destroy the flora and any fauna associated with it; or areas where genuinely endangered creatures or plants may not survive for much longer.

Such sites may need full Nature Reserve protection and may be so specialist that no change can be allowed without specific agreement of genuine authorities on the subject who could predict with accuracy the consequences of the proposed disturbance. A watertight, comprehensive Management Agreement of full owner-ship, by the nation, may be unavoidable in such cases although I still hold the view that, in our property-owning society, Englishmen's homes should be their castles. When compulsory purchase is unavoidable, it is a stricture of the NCC's poor public relations and powers of 'selling' the virtue of conservation, because more owners would co-operate willingly if treated with respect and as partners, instead of being *told* what they can and cannot do on their own land.

Second priority are Sites of Special Scientific Interest where, as I said in the previous chapter, it is really vital that the NCC changes its arrogant policy of refusing to divulge the criteria by which such sites are assessed – which I know, from bitter personal experience, alienates even those with common aims.

The 'specialists' who are involved in this work can get so specialised that they can't see the wood for the trees, knowing more and more about less and less. Change, in the countryside, is another name for evolution, and although we may be able to slow the change temporarily, it is often impossible either to halt or reverse it. So there is a danger of sterilising a whole area for the sake of some minor rarity which may be of importance only to the researcher involved.

The point was illustrated vividly when I took a party of high-powered natural-ists round my wood, mainly to see the deer. One disappeared from the party – and the deer disappeared over the horizon. The explanation proved to be that she had got her PhD for research on an obscure beetle which lives in the bracket fungus on birch trees. Spotting what she thought was a likely bit of habitat, she dived, unbidden, into a thicket – and blew my chances of showing her companions the deer which they had come forty miles to see. She was utterly unrepentant, since birch bracket fungus beetles were far more important, in her eyes, than any herd of deer. It went to show what different values even experts have!

At present, there are over 4000 SSSIs in the country so that their compulsory

purchase would be impractical, either on financial or political grounds. Their success or failure therefore depends almost entirely on the goodwill of those who own or work in them, because the bureaucrats involved in their organisation have fortunately not yet graduated from our servants to our masters so cannot *enforce* their wishes. Their task is confined to 'selling' the doctrine that wildlife conservation is worthwhile, something they cannot do by keeping their cards so close to their chests that nobody else can read their hand.

The third category of site which may be worth encouraging are the minor ones, like mine, which may seem of little scientific interest to the boffins, but which have two potential virtues – the one practical and the other political.

Since SSSIs are obviously limited in number (4000 is not many, spread across the land), they inevitably occupy 'island' sites which may be miles apart, with no physical communication between them. (William Prestwood made this point strongly on page 152). One of the main objections to the removal of hedgerows, apart from the fact that it unbalances the view, is that hedgerows are natural routes of communication, sheltering many animals as they cross hostile country.

A series of small reserves, like mine, could act as vitally important 'stepping stones' for communication between sites which could add enormously to the value of more conventional and officially-designated reserves. But subsidising conservation, in a climate of government spending cuts, can have only limited potential.

I believe, however, that literally hundreds of people would love to do what has given me so much pleasure for so many years, and the same principles apply, whether the wildlife is in an overgrown suburban garden or an uneconomic wood. I have demonstrated that it is possible, with a little innovation and scheming, to generate what cash is needed for very exciting experiments – which I have deliberately developed further than most folk would be inclined to do, simply to prove that it is possible. Any profit I make is ploughed straight back so that I have not pouched a penny from the public purse. Nor do I intend to do so.

But, when I tumble off my perch, there is every prospect that my lifetime's labour of love will be destroyed by taxes. Inheritance Tax, the modern name for Capital Transfer Tax and Death Duties which smelled no sweeter, could force my successors to sell to the highest bidder, who could well be some Flash Harry who would exterminate my beloved wildlife as 'vermin' so that he could cut a status-symbol dash with pheasants.

Having lived to see my wilderness bloom, I should like to think my successors would see the flowers seed. So, although it would be too late to benefit me personally, it would not seem unreasonable if 'stepping stone' sites like this, could be exempt from Inheritance Tax, as Sites of Special Scientific Interest are. This would save them from disintegrating every time an owner died, the benefit being to wildlife, not the owner. I suggest that such sites should remain exempt only so long as their management was sharp enough to maintain the wildlife for which they were created. It would please politicians by collecting the escalating votes of the so-called Green lobby and, far more important in my eyes, it would be more beneficial to wildlife in the future than abortive attempts to play King Canute who tried, in vain, to stem an unstoppable tide.

ent changes in the
tryside, such as prairies of
, have produced effects with
h wildlife cannot keep up

56. AUDIT

I often lie in bed, with the moon as my candle, counting the treasure that Jess and I have amassed during our stewardship of our beloved wilderness. No miser, totting up his hoard of gold, could reap more pleasure than we derive from ours — although it is hardly worth a dime in the hard cash which is too often the counterfeit that passes for success.

The jewels in our hoard are wild birds and beasts we could not coerce to come, but which have accepted our invitation to bed and board with us entirely of their own free will. Some of them 'sing for their supper' with unconventional tunes which are nonetheless music in our ears. A hundred yards away, at the edge of Holly Covert, the early summer air is ripped apart by ribald, belching calls of nesting herons, their chorus having swelled sixfold since we came here in 1963. Below the open bedroom window, we often hear a soft and rhythmic rasping sound which tells us that wild fallow deer are no more than a few feet away, cropping the sweet herbage of the paddock which was no more than a desert of coarse indigestible feggy grass when we arrived.

By far the greatest thrill for me is provided by the small social group of badgers which breed and feed within a stone's throw of the Lodge because, during the last decade, I have joined wholeheartedly with those who have encouraged heavier sentences for those guilty of the obscene crime of badger digging and then baiting with dogs, and the equally obscene campaign of extermination, on entirely spurious evidence, by the Minister of Agriculture and his megalomaniac scientists. There is some satisfaction in being a small cog in the wheel of public revulsion that has eased badgers' lot against their tyrants as well as having made life pleasanter — and safer — for the small colony across the paddock from our house.

When we came, the air was often vibrant with the liquid voices of nuthatches, coloured like faded kingfishers — but more than making up for an undistinguished appearance with their limpid song. Soon after we came, they all vanished, though their disappearance seems to have had nothing to do with us because friends visiting the woodland six miles to the north-east reported a similar loss. We never did discover the cause of their departure. Last season, we saw a pair towards the end of winter but they disappeared before the nesting season. This winter they were on the fat for several hours a day during the weeks of hard weather, and we are living in high hopes that, even if they spurn the nest boxes we have put up for them, they will find natural holes in the trees for themselves.

Grasshopper warblers and nightjars were plentiful in the rough ground left where trees were felled for softwoods to be planted twenty years ago, and their retreat was certainly due to the change of breeding habitat when the pines matured. Now that I have a licence from the Forestry Commission to thin the pines and replace them with native English broad-leaved trees, I am hoping that the restored habitat will attract them back — and perhaps redstarts, too.

That is the joy of such work. The landscape is always changing because the

RIGHT
With Jess on the front lawn

balance of nature is a myth, and chaps like me can give it a deliberate nudge onto a slightly different course and so provide conditions which will favour wild-life that is suffering through more conventional 'progress'.

A criticism often levelled at me is that I am 'playing God' and what right have I to decide that carrion crows, or other enemies of wildlife weaklings, should be snuffed out so that others can live? My answer is that because my management in favour of threatened species is deliberate, it helps to redress the damage caused by 'progress' which is no less effective because it is accidental. Modern farming techniques of hedge removal and chemical pest control have decimated many harmless species of bird, plant and insect. What I try to do is to restore their chances by providing suitable habitat in my wilderness and taking steps to see that the strong do not always benefit at the expense of the weak.

Some of my experiments are still in the pipeline and it is more than possible that their success or failure will only be able to be judged by my successors. The badger sett in front of the window, for instance, has been a roaring success – but its very triumph may spell its downfall.

I constructed the foundation by bulldozing a pile of roots together and covering them with soil so that badgers would open up a sett, to their own design, amongst the crevices (*see* page 136). But they are such formidable excavators that they have thrown out huge mountains of spoil until it must be like a honeycomb inside, which may cause the tunnels to subside and collapse.

Our soil is too damp and puggy for them to find acceptable alternative sites in the wood for themselves which explains why they commuted nightly from their setts on my neighbour's well-drained sandy banks before we came but he doesn't want them back. If I find no alternative accommodation, they may be forced to seek lodgings with a less hospitable host.

This summer, therefore, I shall 'tidy' the wood by dragging a few dozen great tree roots, relics of previous fellings, behind my ancient tractor. I shall place them cunningly in sight of the sitting-room window and use some of the Christmas tree cash to hire Bill Durose and his JCB to cover them with a deep mound of soil. If all goes according to plan, the rabbits will soon move in, followed, perhaps, by a vixen – and then will come the crunch. When the present sett collapses, to become a badger slum, I have my fingers crossed that the tenants will move across the ride to take advantage of the Mod Cons I will have provided – and, this time, where we can view in comfort.

Not everything has worked out so well. Holly Covert is still an open, draughty wood except for isolated small patches of regeneration started by the rooting pigs. I had to be very careful not to put too many in because a herd of pigs, all rooting with bulldozer snouts, could have moved such mountains of soil that they could have annihilated all the wildflowers and young saplings in their path, which would have been counter-productive. By waiting for the acorn fall to take the edge off their appetites, I persuaded them to be more selective about what and where they dug but, in hindsight, it is obvious I was over-cautious. Hitting the right balance was a matter of trial and error, so I asked the NCC for advice and they promised to send a man. That was in 1972, and I am still waiting.